DATE D

The Currency Ratio
in Developing Countries

**PRAEGER SPECIAL STUDIES IN
INTERNATIONAL ECONOMICS AND DEVELOPMENT**

The Currency Ratio
in Developing Countries

Joseph

J. Daniel Khazzoom

FREDERICK A. PRAEGER, Publishers
New York · Washington · London

The purpose of the Praeger Special Studies is to make specialized research monographs in U.S. and international economics and politics available to the academic, business, and government communities. For further information, write to the Special Projects Division, Frederick A. Praeger, Publishers, 111 Fourth Avenue, New York, N.Y. 10003.

FREDERICK A. PRAEGER, PUBLISHERS
111 Fourth Avenue, New York, N.Y. 10003, U.S.A.
77-79 Charlotte Street, London W.1, England

Published in the United States of America in 1966
by Frederick A. Praeger, Inc., Publishers

Library of Congress Catalog Card Number: 66-17360

Printed in the United States of America

TO MY PARENTS

ACKNOWLEDGMENTS

This work owes a great deal to the Research Department of the International Monetary Fund for financing the initial stages of the study and for generously providing the help needed for gathering and processing the basic information for the study. Without the help of the IMF and particularly that of Oscar Altman, Deputy Director of the Research Department, this book would not have been possible.

Subsequent work on the project was supported by the Faculty Research Committee at Cornell University. The Department of Economics did its best to provide additional help; I owe thanks to its chairman, Frank Golay. A grant from the Faculty Research Committee and the Graduate School of Arts and Sciences at New York University financed the last stages of the project.

Many have contributed to this work. I owe a special debt to Seymour E. Harris, now at the University of California, La Jolla, and to Edward Mason, James Duesenberry, and Simon Kuznets of Harvard University for the time they gave so generously in discussing the ideas of the study at its early stages. William White and Graeme Dorrance of the IMF Research Department and my colleague at Cornell, George Staller, have also contributed a great deal of their time in commenting on various parts of the manuscript. Althea MacDonald of the Finance Division of the IMF worked patiently on compiling components and constructing the various series, and Leonard Harris of the Special Studies Division of the IMF wrote the program and supervised the computations. Robert Blakeley (MIT), Vicentte Valdepenas (Cornell), and Martin Greenfield have also helped in the research in various ways. Maria Beer, Doris Tetor, Joan Nowak, and Lillian Weiss did a careful job of typing the manuscript at various stages.

To all of these I owe a debt of gratitude.

J. Daniel Khazzoom

May, 1966
Yonkers, New York

CONTENTS

		Page
ACKNOWLEDGMENTS		vii
LIST OF TABLES		xiii
LIST OF CHARTS		xv

PART I

Chapter

1   THE CURRENCY RATIO AND ITS ECONOMIC
       SIGNIFICANCE   3

       Influence on the Money Supply   3
       Relationship with Velocity   4
       Purpose and Scope of the Study   5
       Footnotes   7

2   THE HYPOTHESES   8

       The Trend   8
       The Level of the Ratio and the
         Stage of Development   9
       The Short-Term Variability   10
       Relationship with Velocity   11
       Footnotes   14

3   THE LITERATURE   16

       The Short-Term Variability of the
         Ratio   16
       The Trend   17
       The Ratio and Velocity   19
       Footnotes   21

4   SELECTED FACTORS IN THE RECENT TREND
       OF THE RATIO   24

       Income per Capita   24
       Monetization   28
       Banking   30
       Inflation   32
       Other Factors   36
       Conclusion   36
       Footnotes   39

PART II. FINDINGS AND CONCLUSIONS

5 THE LEVEL OF THE RATIO   49

   The Cross Section   49
   The Level and the Stage of
      Development   54
   Remark on the Proper Ratio of
      Observation   57
   Conclusion   57
   Footnotes   60

6 THE TREND   62

   Nature of the Trend and Distribution
      of the Rate of Change in the Postwar
      Period   62
   The Level of the Currency Ratio and
      the Rate of Change   67
   Remark on the Relationship with
      Growth   69
   Conclusions for the Postwar Observa-
      tions   70
   Footnotes   73

7 THE TREND--CONTINUED   76

   Inference: Postwar Series   76
   The 1936-62 Series   77
   Concluding Remarks   79
   Footnotes   82

8 VARIABILITY AND RELATIONSHIP WITH
   VELOCITY   86

   Short-Term Variability of the Ratio   86
   Relationship with Velocity   90
   Footnotes   97

PART III

9 SUMMARY   101

APPENDIX A   109

   Deposits Other than Demand Deposits
      and Their Inclusion in the Money
      Supply
   The "Efficiency" Measure

Page

APPENDIX B   123

    Data for the 1948-62 Period, Sources
      and Notes

APPENDIX C   147

    Data for the 1936-62 Period, and
      Source

APPENDIX D   153

    Currency Ratio Charts for the 1948-62
      Period

APPENDIX E   161

    Currency Ratio Charts for the 1936-62
      Period

ABOUT THE AUTHOR   165

LIST OF TABLES

Table   Page

I.1   Frequency Distribution of the Range
       of Values of the Correlation
       Coefficients--Computed from c_1,
       c_2, and COL, 1948-62   34

II.1   Rank of the Last Two-Year Averages of
       c_1 and c_2 50

II.2   Distribution by Geographic Areas of
       the Annual Rate of Change, Computed
       from c_1, c_2, c_3, and c_4 , 1948-62   64

II.3   Distribution of the Efficiency
       Statistic, R_4, Computed From c_1,
       c_2, c_3, and c_4, 1948-62   88

II.4   Correlation Results for the De-
       trended Series and Income Velocity
       of Money   91

               TABLES IN THE APPENDIX

A-1   Frequency Distribution of the Annual
       Rate of Growth of the Percentages of
       Savings and Time Deposits to the
       Money Supply, 1948-62   115

A-2   Frequency Distribution of the Two-Year
       Averages of the Ratio of Savings
       and Time Deposits to the Money Supply   115

A-3   Frequency Distribution of the Annual
       Rate of Growth of the Percentages of
       Savings and Time Deposits to Demand
       Deposits, 1948-62   116

A-4   Frequency Distribution of the Two-
       Year Averages of the Ratio of
       Savings and Time Deposits to Demand
       Deposits, 1961-62   116

B-1   Currency Ratio 1948-62   128

       Supplement to Table B-1   130

Table   Page

B-2   Regression Coefficient of the Trend of
        the Currency Ratio, and the t Value
        of the Logarithms of the Regression
        Coefficient   132

B-3   Preliminary Variables R_1, R_2, R_3,
        Used for the Computations of the
        "Efficiency" of the Series   134

B-4 R_4, R_5--Indices of the "Efficiency"
        of the Series   136

B-5   Coefficients of Linear Correlation
        Computed From c_1, and PCI Index,
        and the Percentage Annual Rate of
        Change of PCI, 1948-61   139

B-6   Correlation Coefficients Computed From
        c_1, c_2, and COL, 1948-62   140

B-7   Savings and Time Deposits as Percen-
        tage of Money Supply   142

B-8   Savings and Time Deposits as Percen-
        tages of Demand Deposits   144

C-1   Currency Ratio, 1936-62   148

C-2   Efficiency Indices, R_4 and R_5, and
        Preliminary Statistics, R_1, R_2, and
        R_3, Used in the Derivation of the
        Indices, 1936-62   150

C-3   Regression Coefficient of the Trend
        of the Currency Ratio, and the t
        Value of the Logarithms of the
        Regression Coefficients, 1936-62   152

LIST OF CHARTS

Chart   Page

II.1   Frequency Densities of Recent Two-
        Year Averages of c_1 and c_2 in
        Thirty-Six Countries   53

II.2   Scatter Diagram of c_1 and c_2 and
        Real Gross National Product per
        Capita in Dollars in Thirty-Three
        Countries   56

II.3   Frequency Densities of the Annual
        Rates of Change of the Currency
        Ratio, 1948-62   66

                CHARTS IN THE APPENDIX

APPENDIX D

    Currency Ratio Charts, 1948-62   154

        Africa   154
        Caribbean and Central America   155
        Europe   156
        Middle East   157
        South America   158
        Southeast Asia   159

APPENDIX E

    Currency Ratio Charts, 1936-62   162

        Africa and Central America   162
        South America   163

PART I

CHAPTER 1

THE CURRENCY RATIO
AND ITS ECONOMIC
SIGNIFICANCE

INFLUENCE ON THE MONEY SUPPLY

The public's demand for currency is an important factor that affects the supply of money. On the basis of fractional reserves, a withdrawal of currency by the public reduces the reserves of the commercial banks, and a flow of currency to the banks adds to their reserves. Unless offset by changes in the banks' excess reserves or by appropriate policy action, an increase in the public's demand for currency leads to a multiple contraction of earning assets and deposits, and a decrease in the public's demand for currency leads to a multiple expansion of earning assets and deposits.

Since, in general, variations in the public's demand for currency are not regulated by policy action, analysis of the change in the public's preference for currency is conveniently made in terms of changes in the currency ratio. By the currency ratio, we mean the currency in circulation outside the banks, taken as a proportion of the money supply.

The relationship between the marginal level of the currency ratio and the potential amount of credit the banking system could extend on the basis of a given increase in the system's reserves is generally expressed in terms of the familiar equation for the money multiplier:

$$k = \frac{1}{c + (1-c)r}$$

where r stands for reserves ratio, and c for marginal currency ratio.[1]

For underdeveloped countries the currency ratio has special significance. Most of these countries are concerned with accelerating their economic growth. Since development funds are short, many have resorted to the alternative of using the central bank's credit to finance investment projects. In the use of this method, the underdeveloped countries have in one respect an advantage over the developed countries: the level of the currency ratio in the underdeveloped countries tends in general to be higher than the level of the ratio in developed countries.[2] Under these conditions, a central bank in an underdeveloped country may expand its monetary liabilities to finance investment projects--directly or indirectly--without running the risk of a large multiple expansion in the money supply.

Two factors may modify these results--secular, as well as short-term changes in the currency ratio. A tendency for the ratio to decrease over time erodes the ability of the central bank to increase its monetary liabilities for financing development projects-- i.e., without letting the resulting increase in the money supply exceed a certain limit, and vice versa. Similarly, the more erratic the short-run behavior of the ratio, the greater is the variability of the resulting increase in the money supply, and the greater is the risk of inflation undertaken by resort to this method, and vice versa.

The problems posed by the short-term variability in the currency ratio are particularly serious for the underdeveloped countries. There are difficulties in forecasting future behavior of the ratio; there are serious limitations on the ability of the central banks in underdeveloped countries to generate swift compensating changes in their monetary liabilities; and there is the fact that commercial banks in these countries tend to hold large amounts of excess reserves. Changes in the central bank's monetary liabilities may be coupled with a combined change in the ratio and in the excess reserves to generate a situation beyond what the central bank can cope with--at least in the short run.

RELATIONSHIP WITH VELOCITY

The significance of the currency ratio in affecting economic activity has long been recognized by economists. R. G. Hawtrey, the British economist, wrote more than five decades ago that by affecting the ability of the bank to extend credit, changes in the currency ratio play a primary role in generating business cycles.[3] In general, investigation of the

relationship between the currency ratio and economic
activity has concentrated on one link in the rela-
tionship--namely, variations in the money supply induced by variations in the ratio.

Money has volume, as well as velocity. A logical extension of the investigation is to examine the
relationship between the currency ratio and this second link--velocity. As behavioral variables, the
currency ratio and the velocity of money may be expected to exhibit a distinct relationship to each
other. And changes in the currency ratio may, not
surprisingly, turn out to influence economic activity, not only through the stock of money, but
through its velocity, as well.

For the underdeveloped countries, this relationship acquires special significance, in view of the
generally heavy reliance on currency for financing
transactions.

PURPOSE AND SCOPE OF THE STUDY

The currency ratio is widely mentioned in the
literature in connection with topics on finance in
the underdeveloped countries. Evidence on the ratio
in these countries, however, is meager, and the discussions are generally based on hypotheses derived
by inference from the developed countries.

In view of the economic significance of the
ratio it would be useful to make available some of
the basic information on the subject, to examine
the validity of some of the hypotheses about the
behavior of the ratio over a wide range of underdeveloped countries, and to explore the possibility
of using the ratio as a tool of economic policy.

The present study is intended for this purpose.
Toward that end, a sample of underdeveloped countries
was chosen, and the series of the currency ratio for
these countries were examined.

The study consists of three parts. Part I--the
present part--begins by discussing the significance
of the ratio. It proceeds to discussion of the hypotheses tested in this study--Chapter Two. This is
followed by a brief examination of the literature on the
subject--Chapter Three. In Chapter Four, an initial at-

tempt is made to analyze the effect of a selected number of factors in the recent trend of the ratio.

Part II has four chapters. They record the results and the conclusions of the statistical tests. A brief exposition of the ratio and the series used in these tests introduces the discussion to this part.

Part III is a summary.

Briefly stated, the following set of hypotheses in relation to the underdeveloped countries are tested in Part II below:

1. The currency ratio has tended to decline over the past.

2. The level of the ratio is inversely related to the level of economic development.

3. In the short run, the currency ratio is variable.

4. Changes in the transactions velocity of money require accommodating changes in the currency ratio.

FOOTNOTES TO CHAPTER ONE

1. This formula is derived in most textbooks on money and banking and much of the literature on the subject. For an illustration, see Richard Goode and Richard S. Thorn, "Variable Reserve Requirements Against Commercial Bank Deposits," IMF Staff Papers, VII (April, 1959), pp. 43-44.

2. For a comparison of the level of the ratio in a sample of 12 countries, including developed and underdeveloped countries, see J. Ahrensdorf and S. Kanesathasan, "Variations in the Money Multiplier and Their Implications for Central Banking," IMF Staff Papers, VIII (November, 1960), Table 1, p. 130. For a larger sample of underdeveloped countries, see Chapter Five below.

3. See R. G. Hawtrey, Currency and Credit (London: Longman's, Green and Co., 1919), pp. 23, 89, 125-26, 376-77. See also his earlier work: Good and Bad Trade (London: Constable and Co., Ltd., 1913), in particular Chapter 15, "The Genesis of Fluctuations," pp. 189-203.

CHAPTER 2

THE TREND

Most discussions involving the currency ratio proceed from the assumption that there is an inverse relationship between economic growth and the trend of the currency ratio. Since, over the past, some economic growth has taken place in the underdeveloped countries, it is generally assumed that the currency ratio in these countries has declined over the past years.

In general, the view that an inverse relationship exists between growth and the trend in the currency ratio focuses on the growth of banks, which, in turn, is associated with economic growth. The idea is simple: As people become more familiar with the general advantages of banking, they tend to hold a larger fraction of their money in the form of deposits. Often, the underlying proposition is narrower: The convenience of using checks as opposed to currency in payments is taken as the key agent that induces people to hold a smaller fraction of their money balances in the form of currency. The decline in the demand for currency becomes then a reflection of the gain in the habit of using checks for payment.

Whatever arguments are advanced in favor of a downward trend in the ratio, the existence of such a trend, as well as its generality, is a matter of fact and can be tested. This is done in Chapters Six and Seven below. In the process, we will deal with the question of whether or not the change in the public's demand for currency in the underdeveloped countries was indeed a mirror image of the change in its habit of using checks in payment. We will find that while in general the demand for currency did decline in the recent past in the underdeveloped countries, the results do not support the assumption that this decline is a reflection of equivalent or necessarily a reflection of parallel gain in the use of checks for payment.

As to the existence of a negative correlation

between growth and the trend of the currency ratio, the proposition, as presented above, concentrates on one factor--namely, banks. Yet there is more than one factor that enters the picture. Economic growth is associated with some developments that tend to exert an upward pressure on the ratio. A priori, there is no obvious reason why the net impact of these developments should always be a downward drift in the ratio. All we could reasonably expect is that the correlation between economic growth--as measured by the income per capita--and the trend of the currency ratio will be at times positive and at times negative.

When the statement is put in this form, it becomes evident that its analytical contribution is limited. Correlation between growth and the trend of the ratio lumps a composite set of relationships and does not give an insight into the nature and the effects of the intermediary factors through which growth operates. And yet, these are the relationships that should be of primary concern to the economist. The same limitation remains when the assumption of inverse relationship is reserved for the long run and abandoned for shorter stretches of time, of, say, a decade or two: The factors through which growth operates, as well as the nature of their association with growth, do not remain the same; furthermore, the effects of these factors on the ratio may also vary in direction.[1]

The proper approach is to go to the underlying factors for analysis. In Chapter Four below, an attempt is made to analyze the effect of selected factors in the trend of the ratio in underdeveloped countries. Unfortunately, serious data problems preclude statistical estimation of the effects of these factors, and the discussion is necessarily tentative. Subsequent tests of hypotheses about relationships with income per capita are first steps in the investigation, but no substitute for the approach advocated. Proper evaluation of the effects of growth on the ratio will unfortunately have to await the needed data on these factors.

THE LEVEL OF THE RATIO AND THE STAGE OF DEVELOPMENT

The hypothesis on the existence of a negative

correlation between growth and the trend in the currency ratio leads to the assumption that the level of the ratio should be inversely related to the degree of economic development. Since income per capita is generally used as a measure of the stage of economic development, the hypothesis could be restated in terms of the existence of negative correlation between the level of the currency ratio and the level of income per capita.

Cross-sectional results are, in general, the product of historic influences. As such they tend to reflect the cumulative effects of those influences that were exerted over a long period of time. Hence, relationships derived from cross-sectional data may, in general, be taken as a reflection of the nature of long-run relationships.[2] To the extent that over the long run, the downward forces associated with growth have, on balance, more than offset the upward forces, we may expect to find a negative correlation between the level of the ratio and the level of income per capita.

THE SHORT-TERM VARIABILITY

The existence of seasonal variations in the ratio has generally been recognized. Other than that, it was generally maintained that the currency ratio is fairly stable in the short run.[3] It is only recently that economists began emphasizing the variable nature of the ratio in the short run.

Short-term variability in the ratio caused by other than seasonal factors may have its source in anxieties and changes in public sentiments which may have no real cause behind them; on the other hand, it may derive from real factors such as economic, political, or demographic changes.[4] Inasmuch as developments of this nature are not rare occurrences in underdeveloped countries, variability in the ratio over the short term should not come as a surprise.

Some empirical work on this subject has already been done;[5] our connection with this aspect of the behavior of the ratio will then be confined to determining the extent of variability of the ratio for a sample larger than the one used to establish the existing results. The measure of variability we will use will also be different from the one that has been used.

RELATIONSHIP WITH VELOCITY

A convenient way for deriving the relationship between the currency ratio and the transactions velocity of money is to make use of Brechling's distinction between active and idle currency, C_a and C_i, respectively.[6] Using similar notations, we write active and idle money balances as M_a and M_i, respectively. Then:

$$(1) \quad C_t = C_{a_t} + C_{i_t} + u_t$$

$$(2) \quad M_t = M_{a_t} + M_{i_t} + v_t$$

Expressing the active and idle currency holdings as a proportion of the active and idle money balances, respectively, we have:

$$(3) \quad \frac{C_a}{M_a} = a$$

$$(3') \quad \frac{C_i}{M_i} = i$$

Using $(M_t - M_{a_t} - v_t)$ for M_{i_t}, substituting for C_a and C_i from (3) and (3') in (1), and dividing through by M_t, we have:

$$(4) \quad c_t = i + (a-i)\frac{M_{a_t}}{M_t} + w_t$$

where c stands for the currency ratio and w_t for $\frac{u_t - iv_t}{M_t}$.

For the short run and under normal conditions, we may reasonably expect the proportions "a" and "i" to remain stable. This assumption will be considered later in the context of inflationary conditions.

For underdeveloped countries, the fraction "a" is likely to be high, and in a number of instances--perhaps a substantial number--it may be practically unity. It is tempting to infer that in these countries "i" is also high, and perhaps very close to "a". This is a possibility; on the other hand, its generality should not be exaggerated. The generally high level of savings and time deposits compared to demand deposits, as well as to the money supply in the underdeveloped countries,[7] does not indicate that the proportion "i" is likely to be predominantly as close to "a" as one may be inclined to believe.

Without loss of generality, we may then take $a > i$.

With these assumptions, and with equation (4)--namely, $c_t = i + (a-i)\frac{M_{at}}{M_t} + w_t$ in mind, it follows that changes in the transactions velocity of money --V_T--should be positively correlated with changes in the currency ratio--c. For inasmuch as an increase in V_T involves activation of idle balances, such increase will be associated with an increase in the ratio $\frac{M_a}{M}$. With $a - i > 0$, an increase in $\frac{M_a}{M}$ entails an increase in c. And vice versa, when V_T declines.

To the extent that the relationship between V_T and V_y --the income velocity of money--is a stable one, we may expect c to correlate positively with V_y, as well. Obviously, the wider the difference between the proportions "a" and "i," the stronger the relationship.

Similar remarks apply to the division of deposits into savings and time deposits, on the one hand, and demand deposits, on the other. Suppose this division parallels the distribution of money balances into active and idle, then the inclusion of savings and time deposits in the definition of the money supply should result in stronger positive correlation between V_y and c, than otherwise. Clearly, the closer the correspondence is, the greater is the improvement in the correlation results.

If the hypothesis presently discussed is valid, and if in fact it is not contradicted by evidence, control of the supply of currency in underdeveloped countries to dampen the rise of velocity emerges as a possible policy measure.[8] This measure may be of great help to central banks in underdeveloped countries, in pursuit of disinflationary monetary policy. Often the velocity rises when the central bank attempts to reduce the money supply or its rate of growth to combat inflation. Restrictive policy which relies on controlling the quantity, as well as the composition of money, could then be more effective in subduing expenditures than policy action which relies solely on the quantity of money.

Could we reasonably expect the parameters "a" and "i" to remain stable in periods of inflation?

The answer for "i" is perhaps easier. This fraction is determined primarily by customs, as well as
by institutions. Since these tend to change very
slowly, it is not unreasonable to expect the fraction
"i" to remain fairly stable in inflationary periods.

The fraction "a," on the other hand, is likely
to rise in inflationary periods. The reason lies
primarily in the induced shift in the composition of
transactions, in favor of those that require wider
acceptability of the means of payments. To amplify
the point: For the majority of people in the underdeveloped countries, the attempt to hedge against inflation consists largely of stepped-up efforts to
hoard food and other essentials, as well as precious
commodities, such as gold and jewelry. Generally,
these commodities are paid for in currency, and
rarely in checks.[9] Hence, a shift in favor of these
commodities may be expected to result in an upward
pressure on the "a" fraction.

There is another mechanism--namely, personal
income tax--which may also prompt an upward pressure
on the "a" fraction in times of inflation. Admit-
tedly, the mechanism may be consequential only in a
limited number of countries. Again, to amplify this
point: By swelling the monetary value of a given
real income, inflation has the effect of increasing
the real burden of personal income tax. This may
induce people to evade the tax. Since it is easier
to conceal transactions financed in currency rather
than in deposits, people may be induced to rely more
heavily on currency for payments, if they want to
evade the heavier tax burden. The effect is likely
to be an upward pressure on the "a" fraction; but,
as mentioned earlier, the effect of the tax mechanism may not be generally consequential, since personal income tax plays a minor role in the tax structure of most of the underdeveloped countries.

In general, then, the fraction "a" is likely to
rise in inflationary periods. To the extent that
increased spending in these periods is financed by
rising velocity, we may expect the over-all currency
ratio--c--to rise faster than we anticipated on the
basis of fixed "a" and "i." This is obvious from
equation (4) above--namely, $c_t = i + (a-i)\dfrac{M_{a_t}}{M_t} + w_t$,

since not only $\dfrac{M_a}{M}$ will increase, but the fraction "a"

as well. Control of the flow of currency in disinflationary periods becomes then the more important for
damping the rising tendency of velocity.

FOOTNOTES TO CHAPTER TWO

1. For example, improvement in communications may
lead to increased monetization and hence to an upward pressure on the currency ratio; on the other
hand, by linking separate parts of the country together, improved communications may encourage increased use of banking facilities or may enhance the
spread of banking in so-far "isolated" communities;
the effect in that case would tend to be a downward
pressure on the currency ratio. In general, both
effects are present simultaneously, but the net impact may differ depending on the specific regions
involved.

2. This is generally the underlying assumption in
econometric studies which use cross-sectional results
to supplement investigations based on time series
analyses.

3. See, for example, J. E. Meade, "The Amount of
Money and the Banking System," Economic Journal,
XLIV (March, 1934), p. 80; See also Erich Schneider,
"The Determinants of the Commercial Banks' Credit
Potential in a Mixed Money System," Banca Nazionale
del Lavoro Quarterly Review, VIII (September, 1955),
p. 133.

4. To give one or two specific instances, in Israel
the behavior of the ratio reflects largely the jerky
inflow of immigrants who came from countries where
banking habits were not developed, and the extent to
which these immigrants were settled in areas far in
the deserts, where banking facilities took time to
reach. In Venezuela (this country was not included
in this study) there was a sudden jump in the ratio
in 1958. The reason for this change lies apparently
in the fear, following the overthrow of Perez-Jimenez,
that bank deposits might be frozen to finance a com-
pulsory loan to the government.

5. J. Ahrensdorf and S. Kanesathasan, "Variations in
the Money Multiplier and Their Implications For
Central Banking," IMF Staff Papers, VIII (November,
1960), pp. 126-45.

6. Acknowledgment to Frank Brechling for comments
and suggestions on this part of the work. Brechling's
idea of extending the Keynesian distinction between
active and passive money balances to currency holdings
was first presented in his article "The Public's

Preference for Cash," Banca Nazionale Del Lavoro
Quarterly Review , XI (September, 1958), p. 380.

7. See Table 7 and 8 of Appendix B.

8. Obviously the operation. of the measure is not
symmetrical. Like monetary policy, it suffers from
the drawback that has been best described by saying
that releasing the string does not necessarily make
the donkey go to drink.

9. My experience in Iraq indicates that for food,
as well as other essentials, this is true even of
wholesale transactions.

CHAPTER **3**   THE LITERATURE

Although the subject of the currency ratio appears frequently in discussions of financial topics
in relation to economic development, no attempt has
yet been made--except in two instances, mentioned
below--to provide empirical content to the subject.
As it is, fragmentary propositions on the behavior
or the ratio, sometimes contradicting each other, are
scattered here and there all through the literature.
In general, they are inferred from observations about
the ratio in the developed countries, and not infrequently, they are only implicit in the discussion.

Even when one comes to the developed countries
one finds very limited empirical work and a good
deal of it appears only as incidental.[1] In view of
the fact that the economic significance of the ratio
has been recognized for so long, it is surprising
that so little work has been done on the subject.
At present, much of the empirical work on the subject
was done during the fifties. Comparatively little
has been done in the present decade.[2]

A brief examination of the literature on the
hypotheses with which this study is concerned will
occupy the rest of this chapter.

THE SHORT-TERM VARIABILITY OF THE RATIO

The variability of the ratio in a few underdeveloped countries over short intervals ranging from
five to ten years was examined in 1958 by Ahrensdorf
and Kanesathasan.[3] The study is mainly concerned
with isolating the contribution of each of the factors affecting the money multiplier--with the currency ratio being one of them. The authors concluded
the evidence contradicts the assumption of short-run
stability of the currency ratio, and recommended ex-
plicit inclusion of the ratio in the analytical frame-
work of monetary analysis.

Ahrensdorf and Kanesathasan's investigation
covers a relatively small group--twelve countries in
all, and only five of these can be categorized as

underdeveloped.[4]

    The measure the authors used for deriving their
conclusion on the variability of the ratio is also
not particularly suited for the purpose. The variability of the ratio is generally used to connote erratic behavior, and it appears that it is also in
this sense that the authors used the term. The coefficient of variation which the authors used is well
suited for measuring the degree of dispersion; on the
other hand, a series may be dispersed but not variable, in the sense of being erratic.[5] In this study,
a different measure of variability is used. It is
termed the "efficiency of the series" and is described in Appendix A below.[6]

                         THE TREND

    No empirical work has been done on the trend of
the ratio in underdeveloped countries. The only information available on the trend derives from charts
for monetary series, including currency ratio series,
that the IMF published in 1951 for forty-eight countries and for periods ranging generally between
1938-50.[7] About half of the countries for which
charts appeared could be categorized as underdeveloped. Other than the pictorial aspect of the publi-
cation, the work has little content.

    Cagan's work on the ratio in the U.S. is well
known. The work is concerned mainly with the secular behavior of the ratio.[8] The period covered is
1879-1955. During that period the ratio tended to
decline.

    For the 1919-55 period Cagan used a double loga-
rithmic function with three explanatory variables:
Expected net rate of interest on deposits; expected
real income per capita; and personal income tax as
percentage of personal income. His results show that
these variables relate to the currency ratio respectively as follows: inversely, inversely, and directly.
The regression equation accounts for 89 per cent of
the variation in the ratio; and, when the three explanatory variables are arranged in decreasing order
of contribution in explaining the behavior of the
ratio, the interest variable comes first, and the tax
variable comes last; the income per capita falls in
between, and contributes almost as little as the tax
variable.[9]

The estimates derived for the 1919-55 period were found consistent with the data for the 1875-1919 period.

In a follow-up article, George Macesich attempted a test of Cagan's hypotheses for the Canadian economy for the 1924-58 period.[10] During that period the currency ratio rose slightly in Canada.

Using Cagan's double logarithmic function, Macesich finds the three variables taken together explain 85 per cent of the variation in the ratio during the 1926-58 period. The sign of the income elasticity coefficient in this equation is positive, and Macesich argues that these results are not conclusive because the income variable is not accurate for the 1926-34 period.[11]

Using the same function with the same three variables for the 1935-58 period, Macesich finds the three variables combined explain 94 per cent of the variations in the ratio, with the elasticity of the tax, the interest, and the income variables being positive, negative, and negative, respectively. Ranked by decreasing order of contribution in explaining the variations in the ratio, the tax variable comes first, the income variable comes last, and the interest variable falls in between with its contribution being close to that of the income.[12]

The results of Cagan's study for the U.S. and Macesich's study for Canada leave much to be desired. To be sure, returns on deposits and tax evasions may be reasonably expected to affect the ratio. What is in question, however, are the high premiums that these results put on interest on deposits in the U.S.,[13] and income tax in Canada. The secular behavior of the currency ratio reflects the effects of factors more fundamental than tax evasion or returns on deposits; and analysis of the secular behavior of the ratio should focus on those institutional factors which shaped this behavior, if it is to contribute to our understanding of the subject. Indeed, one can hardly disagree with McDonald's remark to the effect that changes in the currency ratio have their basic causes in structural changes in the economy, and that it is only by analyzing these basic causes that we gain better understanding of the behavior of the ratio.[14]

Why is it, one may wonder, that the results of
the two studies put such high premium on the interest,
in the case of U.S., and on the income tax, in the
case of Canada? Statistically, the answer may be in
the use of the income per capita as a proxy variable
for the underlying factors that affect the behavior
of the ratio. Had the actual variables--for which
the income per capita stands--appeared explicitly in
the equation, doubtless the effect of interest in
the U.S. and income tax in Canada would have been reduced.

Economists do in general resort to the use of
broad variables, such as the income per capita as a
proxy for variables on which time series are not readily available. The method has limitations, and the
cost incurred in deriving the neat statistical results
in a multivariate estimating function should not be
underestimated. I have pointed out earlier that the
use of income per capita in gross correlation analysis
does not reveal the underlying relationships. Further,
as I indicate in the next chapter, the use of this
variable in a partial correlation analysis yields
tautological and sometimes misleading results.

All too often, however, "omnibus" variables are
seized upon with little concern to their appropriate-
ness and to the meaningfulness of their results; and
this brings the search to an end when it has hardly
begun. On this point, Macesich's approach is illustrative.[15] It is also relevant to note that his
double logarithmic function for the 1935-58 period
yielded an income elasticity of -0.099. Judging by
the size of the standard error of this coefficient,
the result can hardly be called significant.[16] How
are we to interpret these results? That the structural changes associated with economic growth had no
significant effect on the currency ratio? And if so,
why? Or is it that they do have significant effects,
but that these effects are of opposite direction and
roughly of equivalent strength? There is nothing
that the income per capita does to enlighten us on
these questions. Macesich does not attempt a clari-
fication either.

THE RATIO AND VELOCITY

The relationship between the currency ratio and
the velocity of money has occupied the attention of

economists very little. This is particularly true
for the underdeveloped countries. No work has been
done on this relationship for the underdeveloped
countries--and for that matter on any aspect of the
behavior of the ratio, except for the IFS's publica-
tion and Ahrensdorf's and Kanesathasan's work mentioned earlier. In the context of developed countries, there have been only two isolated instances
in which this relationship has been dealt with--
Wilson's and Brechling's work of the late fifties.[17]

Wilson demonstrated that in the 1921-56 period
bank deposits in the U.K. have been a highly variable
proportion of the GNP, while currency remained a
fairly stable proportion of the GNP for the same period.[18] From this he inferred that greater volume
of monetary expenditures cannot be made possible by
increases in velocity alone, unless accompanied by
an increase in the currency in circulation. Hence,
he recommends to control the issue of currency, instead of concentrating attention on deposits, in
order to prevent velocity from rising and financing
increased expenditures.

Wilson makes no attempt to provide an analytical
background to his case, and his conclusion rests
purely on empirical evidence.

It remained for Frank Brechling to propose an
analytical link between velocity and the currency
ratio.[19] The link rests on the distinction between
active and passive currency balances, and comes as
a by-product of his attempt to analyze the effect
of the short-term variations in the ratio upon the
supply of money.

Brechling tested for direct relationship between
the currency ratio and the velocity of money on a
group of eight Western countries.[20] His series begin in 1950 and cover eight to nine years. In general, the series reveal conformity in the year to year
movements of the ratio and velocity, and Brechling
concluded, hesitantly though, that a policy of controlling the issue of currency coupled with a policy
of controlling the money supply may be more effective
than concentration on the latter.

We shall examine the empirical evidence on the
relationship between the currency ratio and velocity
in Part II. We stop at this juncture to examine selected factors that may have affected the recent
trend in the currency ratio.

FOOTNOTES TO CHAPTER THREE

1. See, for example, the discussion of the trend of the ratio in France by H. Fourmier, "The Problem of Controlling Liquidity in France," Banca Nazionale del Lavoro Quarterly Review, XIII (December, 1960), pp. 317-33, in particular p. 322.

2. In the following studies, except where indicated, the authors exclude savings and time deposits from the definition of the money supply.

3. Ahrensdorf and Kanesathasan, op. cit., pp. 126-45.

4. These are Brazil, Ceylon, Colombia, Egypt, and the Philippines. The remaining seven are: Canada, West Germany, Italy, Japan, New Zealand, U.K., and U.S.

5. The coefficient of variation is derived by dividing the standard deviation by the mean.
    Suppose now we have the following two series:
    A.   35.5, 35.0, 34.5, 35.0, 35.5, 35.0, 34.5
    B.   36.5, 36.0, 35.5, 35.0, 34.5, 34.0, 33.5
Series A is erratic; series B is smooth. On the other hand, series A is concentrated around 35.0; series B is more dispersed around the same mean. The coefficient of variation will be larger for B than for A. As a gauge of dispersion, the measure is correct. As a gauge of variability, the measure is wrong, since A is erratic while B is not.

6. Brechling challenged the assumption of short-term stability of the ratio in developed countries. His results are based on an examination of the behavior of the ratio in eight Western countries for a period of eight to nine years during the fifties. Brechling's work was mainly concerned with the effect of variations in the ratio upon the money supply. See Frank Brechling, "The Public's Preference for Cash," Banca Nazionale del Lavoro Quarterly Review, XI (September, 1958), pp. 377-93.
    Mention should also be made in this connection of MacDonald's work on the internal drain in the U.S. during the period 1914-52, and his later work on the factors behind the behavioral pattern of the currency ratio in the U.S. during the 1940-53 period. See, Stephen L. MacDonald, "The Internal Drain and Bank Credit Expansion," and "Some Factors Affecting the Increased Relative Use of Currency Since 1939," The Journal of Finance, VIII (December, 1953), pp. 407-21, and XI (September, 1956), pp. 313-27, respectively.

7.   IMF, International Financial Statistics, IV
(September, 1951), pp. iii-vii.

8.   Phillip Cagan, "The Demand for Currency Relative
To The Total Money Supply," Journal of Political
Economy, LXVI (August, 1958), pp. 301-28. The
study appeared also in 1958 with a statistical appendix as Occasional Paper No. 62 of the National Bureau of Economic Research.
     Cagan's definition of the money supply includes
time deposits of all commercial banks held by the
non-banking public.

9.   The coefficients of partial determination are
69 per cent, 47 per cent, 43 per cent, for the interest, income, and tax variables, respectively.
Ibid., p. 323, footnote 8.

10. George Macesich, "Demand for Currency and
Taxation in Canada," Southern Economic Journal,
XXXIX (July, 1962), pp. 33-8.
     Macesich does not report how he defines the
money supply, but I presume he includes time deposits in the definition.

11. Ibid., p. 35.

12. The coefficient of partial determination is
87 per cent, 18 per cent, and 14 per cent for the
tax, interest, and income variable. Ibid., p. 35.

13. In Cagan's results, variations in the interest
on deposits alone explain 79 per cent of the variations.

14. MacDonald, "The Internal Drain and Bank Credit
Expansion," p. 418.

15. Macesich does not make serious efforts to look
into the nature of the relationships between the
currency ratio and the factors that may have affected
its secular behavior in Canada. He accepts Cagan's
judgment--which Cagan made about the series in the
U.S.--that many of the factors that affected the
ratio had negligible influence and that others "May
be collapsed into single variables." Macesich, op.
cit., p. 33.

16. The standard error is 0.054--i.e., a little
above half the size of the elasticity coefficient.

17.   Thomas Wilson, "The Rate of Interest and Monetary Policy," Oxford Economic Papers, IX (October,
1957), pp. 235-60; and Frank Brechling, "The Public's
Preference for Cash," Banca Nazionale del Lavoro
Quarterly Review, XI (September, 1958), pp. 377-93.

18.   Wilson, op. cit., pp. 246, 248.

19.   Brechling, op. cit., pp. 377-93.

20.   Canada, England, France, Italy, Netherlands,
Sweden, U.S.A. and West Germany.
     The consistency in the definitions of Brechling's
money supply series may be open to question, as
Brechling points out, since the series he uses are
derived from different sources for different countries.

CHAPTER **4**   SELECTED FACTORS IN
                                 THE RECENT TREND OF
                                 THE RATIO

The behavior of the currency ratio is influenced
by a large number of factors that cover a wide range
in the social spectrum: economic, political, anthro-
pological, and sociological.

In terms of the nature of their effects, these
factors may be broadly classified as short-term and
long-term. This distinction is not always possible
to make, however, and at times the same factor may
play simultaneously a long-, as well as a short-term
role.

In terms of the direction of their effects,
these factors may be generally classified as those
that tend to exert an upward pressure on the currency
ratio, on the one hand, and those that tend to exert
a downward pressure on the ratio, on the other. Here
again, the distinction is not hard and fast, and the
same factor may appear at one time under one category,
and at another time under the opposite category.

In the present chapter we explore a selected
number of factors in the trend of the ratio and ex-
pound a few hypotheses, but the discussion is only
a first step. The lacunae of evidence on the factors
considered precludes proper assessment of their role,
and the analysis is necessarily tentative. The next
step would have to proceed in the direction of first
removing the obstacle posed by the lack of data on
the relevant factors; for without adequate evidence,
there is no basis on which to judge the significance
of these factors.

We dispose first of the factor that is most
frequently mentioned--namely, income per capita.

INCOME PER CAPITA

The view that an inverse relationship exists
between economic growth and the trend in the cur-

rency ratio was discussed earlier. It was noted that this view generally focuses on the effect of growth of banks associated with economic growth.

Sometimes, discussions involving the income per capita use this variable in the sense of personal income. Generally, the arguments about the existence of inverse relationship, between the currency ratio and the per capita income--using the variable in the sense of personal income--are not thoroughly worked out. What is important, however, is that basic to these arguments is the assumption that banking ser- vices are readily available. The assumption is not applicable to most of the underdeveloped countries. Alternatively, I have argued that the use of the gross correlation between income per capita--used as proxy for the factors associated with economic growth --and the currency ratio does not yield insightful results on the relationships that the analysis should be concerned with.

Since in some of the studies of the ratio, the relationship between the income per capita and the currency ratio appears in the context of a multi- variate equation--that is, in the sense of partial correlation--I turn to a brief exposition of the dif- ficulties of the partial correlation method and the nature of the results it yields.

The Partial Correlation Method

The results derived by this method follow by virtue of: (1) the logic of the operation for de- riving the partial correlation; and, when the income per capita is used as a proxy variable, (2) the choice of the factors which the income per capita is made to stand for.

As such the results are tautological. They could also be misleading. The pitfall is that their nature can be easily overlooked.

To fix ideas, let us use the simple device of grouping the factors that affect the secular behavior of the currency ratio into two categories: A and B.[1]

Under category A we include all those factors which we expect to be (1) directly related to the income per capita but inversely to the currency ra- tio or (2) inversely related to the income per capita but directly to the currency ratio.

Under category B we include all those factors which we expect to be (1) directly related to the income per capita, as well as to the currency ratio, or (2) inversely related to income per capita, as well as to the currency ratio.

Consider a country in which the income per capita has been growing over time. The existence of a negative partial correlation between the income per capita, on the one hand, and the currency ratio, on the other, means essentially the following: If we remove from the observed behavior of the currency ratio, the upward effect attributable to the factors in category B, and then correlate the remainder with the income per capita,[2] the resulting coefficient will have a negative sign. This result will generally hold by virtue of the fact that we have used the income per capita as a proxy variable for the factors in category A; and since the effect of these factors has been, as income per capita grew, to exert a downward pressure on the currency ratio, we may reasonably expect this downward effect to be reflected in our results as a negative partial correlation between the income per capita and the currency ratio. Hence, the negative sign we obtained is simply a consequence of the logic of the operation for deriving the partial correlation coefficient, as well as our own decision on what the income per capita should stand for.

By the same token, we could first take into account the effect of the factors in category A, and let the income per capita stand for the factors in category B. We may then reasonably expect the sign of the partial correlation coefficient to be positive, rather than negative.

The results of the partial correlation with income per capita should, then, not come as a surprise, for they are our own making. Indeed what we are actually doing amounts to the same thing as defining income per capita in such a way that certain results will follow, and then proceeding to derive these results formally. Needless to add that such results are tautological.

One related problem may compound the difficulty --namely, the deceptive effect that the similarity in the definition of income per capita may have on the interpretation of the results.

To amplify this point, as a proxy variable, income per capita may be used in different investigations of the same subject for different countries to represent different sets of factors. The partial correlation results derived in each instance may be different. But these results cannot be taken to mean necessarily that the effect of economic growth on the dependent variable has been different, even though the income per capita may have been constructed in exactly the same manner in each case. The point is that the results of the correlation are not comparable because what the income per capita stands for is not the same in each instance. In other words, despite the fact that in both cases the variable is called by the same name, and is also defined similarly, it is not really the same animal.

It is not always that the nature of this dual aspect of the use of income per capita is recognized, and results derived with the income per capita used in different contexts are not infrequently treated as comparable and interpreted accordingly.[3]

Conclusion

To recapitulate, the sign of the partial correlation coefficient of the income per capita with the currency ratio is a consequence of the choice of the category for which the income per capita is made to stand for. As such, the results are tautological. They could also be misleading. The logical conclusion is evident: The analysis of the behavior of the currency ratio should be attempted in terms of the individual factors that directly influence the ratio, rather than in terms of the broad variable income per capita. From the statistical, as well as the economic point of view, the results derived by this approach will be more meaningful and less susceptible to misinterpretations. This just underscores the importance of constructing the required series on the relevant factors.

MONETIZATION

The Impact

The process of monetization may have been for many underdeveloped countries the most significant factor in influencing the recent trend of the currency ratio. Many of these countries, possibly more so Asiatic and African than Latin American, have large barter areas which have been and are still undergoing the process of monetization.

The impact of monetization is likely to be an upward pressure on the currency ratio. This is so for two reasons: One is that generally no banks exist in the newly monetized sectors and none are likely to go there before such sectors become well integrated in the monetized part of the economy. Under the circumstances, the only choice a person has, if he wants to build up his cash balances, is to hold currency. Second, there are psychological problems in the transition from a stage of barter, where the commodities exchanged provide tangible evidence of security, to such less tangible source such as bank account. The transfer to currency is in itself enough of a big step to require a halt on the way. As a matter of fact, the evidence, limited as it is, indicates that people at this stage tend to prefer coin over banknotes--most likely because the former has obvious intrinsic value, while the latter does not.

Rate and Measurability

The rate of monetization, and, hence, the consequent demand for currency it generates, is affected mainly by two variables: the size of the non-monetized sector and the policies adopted by the authorities. That is to say, other things being equal, the extent of monetization is likely to be larger when the non-monetized sector is larger, and, for a given size of non-monetized sector, the more the efforts of development are geared to non-monetized areas the faster is monetization likely to proceed.

There are difficult conceptual problems in determining the rate of monetization, and in assessing the quantitative effect of the process on the currency ratio. The practical problems are even more difficult.

Considering alternative methods, it seems that it would be best to use the change in the volume of barter as an indicator of the additional demand for currency, generated by monetization.[4] Even here, however, certain adjustments have to be made. One, to allow for the upward pressure on the size of the non-monetized sector exerted by the expansion of the population in this sector. If no account is taken of this factor, the measure will consistently--but not necessarily uniformly--underestimate the extent of monetization and hence the consequent upward pressure the process has exerted on the currency ratio. Secondly, depending on the extensiveness of the production estimates for the barter areas, the measure may have to be adjusted in order to take account of the change in the amount of production for own use.[5]

From the practical end, there is no adequate evidence on the significance of the non-monetized sector in the economies of underdeveloped countries.[6] On the face of it, it looked in some limited instances as if the methods used in estimating the size of the non-monetized production for national income accounts purposes were acceptable. Close investigations of these instances revealed that, contrary to impression, the estimates are generally speculative.[7]

The author's search for a suitable indicator of the size of the non-monetized sector has not yet yielded worthwhile results.

With the state of data being as it is, an examination of the nature of development policies adopted in the different countries could shed some light on the question. Unfortunately, the search in this direction did not lead much further.

Many experts agree that development policies in Southeast Asia have, on the whole, tended to be geared more to the poorer rural areas than were their counterparts in Latin America.[8] To the extent this is true, it may be an indication that monetization was more significant a factor in the recent trend of the ratio in Southeast Asia than in Latin America. But this still leaves us in the dark about the situation in the other parts of the world.

BANKING

The Role of the Banks

Inasmuch as the availability of outlet for holding money, in forms other than currency, may set a limit on the extent of the decline in the currency ratio, the growth of banks is probably the most important single determinant of the level of the currency ratio.

Four major factors affect the efficacy of a bank in attracting deposits. These are the nature of ownership, the geographic location of the institution, its size, and its standard of honesty and efficiency in business. Within these constraints, the downward effect of the growth of banks on the currency ratio may vary within a wide range.

The significance of the last two factors is evident. A word or two on the first two is in order.

Nature of Ownership

By referring to the nature of ownership, I mean to distinguish between foreign banks on the one hand, and indigenous banks, on the other.[9] On some counts, foreign banks may be more effective in attracting deposits than indigenous banks; on some others, they may not. Foreign banks generally have the backing of well established large institutions abroad. This may be a source of confidence for potential depositors. On the other hand, foreign banks tend to concentrate on financing trade or, even more narrowly, exports. This may discourage the prospective depositor who wants to count on his bank's assistance in times of need. Furthermore, people in many countries tend to be hostile to foreigners and to the idea of foreign ownership of banks.[10] In some cases this aversion extends itself to minority groups which may predominate in the financial field, even though such groups have been residents of the same country for a long time.[11] In either case, hostile attitude toward the owners of the bank may limit its attractiveness.

Geographic Location

Banks in underdeveloped countries tend to conglomerate in geographically limited areas. Specifically, commercial banks tend to concentrate on the larger towns and, not infrequently, crowd themselves in one single street of the town. A bank added to a big conglomeration of banks may divert to itself part of the deposits held at other banks and accommodate the needs of new depositors, as well. Evidently, some downward pressure on the currency ratio will result. If the same bank is established in an area where no banking facilities have so far existed, it may or may not be able to attract as many depositors. But in terms of its effect on the currency ratio, the downward pressure it exerts may be stronger only if the amount of deposits attracted in the isolated locality will be larger than the amount of new deposits which could otherwise be attracted in the city. Other things related to the bank itself being equal, the outcome is contingent upon a number of considerations: cultural traits of the inhabitants of the locality, the level of income, the density of the population, and the communication facilities.

It is possible to quantify the significance of the factors in the attractiveness of a bank, and hence, to determine their contribution to the trend of the currency ratio in the recent past.[12] Currently, there is no trace of evidence in the literature on the ingredients needed for such quantification.

The Role of Private Banks

For essentially two reasons, one may venture the hypothesis that the role played by the private banks in bringing down the currency ratio could not have been--and is not likely to be in the foreseeable future--as significant in the underdeveloped countries as it has been historically in most Western countries.

One reason is connected with the peculiarities of the private banks in the underdeveloped countries, which make it difficult for these banks to attract adequate funds to finance large-scale industrialization. For most countries, this role has been played largely by public and semi-public financial institutions. And inasmuch as the private banks of the underdeveloped countries occupy a less prominent place in finance activities in comparison with their peers of the earlier times--when the economically advanced countries were at a similar stage of development--most likely their contribution to the downward pressure on the currency ratio has been comparatively less significant, as well.[13]

A second reason is related to the attitude toward private enterprise, as reflected in the pattern of economic development that the underdeveloped countries have chosen for themselves--namely, the development along socialistic rather than private lines. This choice reflects largely an adverse attitude toward private enterprise, which, in turn, may have its roots in philosophical indoctrination or in unfortunate experience with colonial rule. Rightly or wrongly, private enterprise tends to be identified with colonial rule. The tendency of people to share in the convictions of their leaders is in this case enhanced by the personal experience many have had with what is generally considered as another symbol of the private enterprise--namely, the money lenders. Under the circumstances, an individual may find it hard not to project his suspicion to the privately-owned bank--an institution that bears a similar label.[14]

INFLATION

Inflation affects the behavior of the currency ratio through essentially three major channels:

1. Shifts in the composition of the transactions in favor of those that require wider acceptability of the means of payment.

2. Personal income tax.

3. Capital flight.

Both the transactions and the tax mechanisms have been discussed in Chapter Two above.[15] We turn to the third channel.

Capital Flight

The term is used here to connote the tendency of people to increase their holdings of foreign exchange assets, at the expense of their holdings of local funds. This includes cases of over-invoicing of imports, under-invoicing of exports, and outright conversion of local funds into foreign exchange assets by legal or illegal means.

There is no worked-out theory of capital flight, and the factors affecting such movements of capital are not clearly understood.[16] Most observers would agree though that the extent of capital flight is largely influenced by the state of confidence of the public--on the economic, as well as the political front. Inasmuch as inflation does affect the confidence of the public in the value of the local money, it is likely that inflationary periods will be associated with an acceleration in the process of conversion of local funds into foreign exchange assets.

Evidence is lacking on the nature of the entities that tend to be involved in this practice. A priori, however, there does not seem to be any reason to believe that the average individual or the small businessman do engage in such activities to any large extent. It seems more reasonable to assume that access to these activities is limited to wealthy individuals and large institutions. These, in turn, tend to constitute a significant proportion of the holders of bank deposits.[17] Accordingly, the immediate impact of capital flight is likely to be an upward pressure on the currency ratio.

What follows the initial impact admits of several combinations of possibilities. But in general, it is likely that, if the inflationary pressures persist for a relatively long time, capital flight will halt or be even reversed. Such halt or reversal may become necessary, in order to meet the minimal financial needs at the higher price level. It may also be induced by subsequent devaluation, and to the extent such development does take place, the upward pressure on the currency ratio will abate or reverse itself.

A crude attempt to examine the nature of co-variation of the currency ratio and the holding of foreign assets in the U.S. for five Latin American countries yielded a mixed pattern. No data could be compiled for the holdings of foreign assets in Europe. Changes in the distribution of these assets among countries might have influenced the results materially.

Synchronism In The Behavior Of The Currency Ratio And The Price Level--Conclusion

In general, therefore, the preceding analysis indicates that the effect of inflation is likely to

Table I.1

Frequency Distribution of the Range of Values of the Correlation Coefficients [a] — Computed from c_1, c_2, and COL [b], 1948-1962 [c]

Range of Correlation Coefficients	$c_{1t}=a+b(COL)_t$	$\log c_{1t}=a+b\log(COL)_t$	Detrended $c_{1t}=a+b(COL)_t$	Detrended $c_{2t}=a+b(COL)_t$	Detrended $\log c_{2t}=a+b\log(COL)_t$	$c_{1t}=a+b(COL)_{t-1}$	$c_{2t}=a+b(COL)_{t-1}$	$\log c_{2t}=a+b\log(COL)_{t-1}$	Detrended $c_{1t}=a+b(COL)_{t-1}$	Detrended $c_{2t}=a+b(COL)_{t-1}$	Detrended $\log c_{2t}=a+b\log(COL)_{t-1}$	Detrended $c_{2t}=a+b(COL)_{t-1}$
-1.00 - -.80	10	10	9	9	9	13	12	10	9	9	8	1
-.79 - -.60	5	4	5	4	5	5	7	9	7	6	6	1
-.59 - -.40	1		1	1	2	6	4	2	2	4		2
-.39 - -.20	3	2	2	4	3	2	2	5		2	4	4
-.19 - 0.00	3	3	3	7	3	2	5	5	9	7		8
.01 - .20		3	1	4	1	2	3	3	6	2	2	6
.21 - .40	6	1	3	9	2		7		6	1	1	4
.41 - .60	2	3	2	2	2	3	6	2	4	1	1	6
.61 - .80	2	2	3	3	2	2	2	1	4	2	1	3
.81 - 1.00	2	2	2	2	3	2	3	1	3	3		5
-1.00 - 0.00	22	14	22	14	20	28	27	13	14	30	20	15
0.01 - 1.00	12	5	12	6	14	6	7	6	20	4	1	19
-1.00 - 1.00	34	19	34	20	34	34	34	19	34	34	21	34

a/ Figures shown under a given row and column represent the number of cases where the value of correlation coefficient, as computed from the equation of the form given under the column heading, fall within the range stated in the given row. Figures raised above the line level represent the number of cases that fall within the same coefficient range, and which were found significant with 95% confidence interval. The reader is cautioned not to put too much emphasis on the results of the significance test, since the observations are time-series.

b/ COL = Cost of living index, with 1953 taken as the base year.

c/ For some countries the period is shorter. For further information on the length of the period, see the detailed table in the Appendix.

be an upward pressure on the currency ratio.[18] In a
few underdeveloped countries growth has been proceeding with reasonable price stability, interrupted
only occasionally by short inflationary spurts.   In
most of the others, however, inflation has been a
chronic feature of economic growth.   In light of the
preceding analysis, it is natural to expect the currency ratio in most underdeveloped countries to have
been subjected to upward pressure on account of the
inflationary factor.   To evaluate properly the significance of this pressure in the recent behavior of
the currency ratio would require evidence on the
other factors that may have affected the ratio.
Since the necessary information is lacking, the results of the alternative tests reported below are
gross in nature, and therefore not necessarily conclusive.   Proper tests of the validity of the hypothesis expounded here will have to await the necessary evidence.

The results of attempts to explore the degree
of synchronism in the behavior of the ratio are recorded in Table B-6, and summarized in Table I.1
below.   The latter is arranged in the form of frequency distribution and gives the range of the correlation coefficients computed for thirty-four countries.[19]

Several types of correlation functions were
examined: linear, as well as non-linear.   In addition correlation coefficients were computed for
de-trended series.[20]

The results reveal a mixed pattern.   Within
this pattern, a tendency for the predominance of
positive correlation may be discerned.   However,
the generality of this pattern is limited.

More specifically, the unadjusted data yield
a predominance of negative correlation--approximately
two-thirds of the total for each of the different correlation types attempted.   The results for these data,
however, incorporate the effects of both trend and
fluctuations.   Elimination of a linear trend yields
an inverted picture with a predominance of cases with
positive correlation in the year to year variations
between the currency ratio and the cost of living index.   This is most obvious in South America for the
de-trended and unlagged variables.   In general, however, where the series were de-trended, and for each

type of correlation attempted, the number of positive coefficients constitutes only three-fifths of the total number of countries included in the sample.

OTHER FACTORS

The exploratory discussion in this chapter is confined to a limited number of factors. A brief note on two other factors--namely, urbanization and income distribution--will close the discussion.

Since banking facilities are relatively limited in the rural areas, urbanization is likely to have the effect of depressing the ratio. Its impact, however, can be taken care of through the geographic factor, when the effect of the banks on the currency ratio is gauged, since urbanization increases the population density in the areas considered.

Income distribution may exert a downward or upward pressure on the currency ratio, depending on whether growth is associated with increase or decrease in the inequality of income distribution, respectively. The underlying assumption is that the higher income groups tend to hold a smaller proportion of their money balances in the form of currency.

Evidence for the developed countries suggests that as economic growth proceeds the inequality of income distribution is reduced.[21] The experience of the developed countries does have bearing upon the economic growth of the underdeveloped countries. On the other hand, there are elements in the presently underdeveloped countries which may have contributed to a widening in the disparity of income distribution.[22] As it is, we do not know whether income inequality moved in one direction or the other in the underdeveloped countries over the recent past.[23]

CONCLUSION

Attempting to bring together the considerations advanced in this chapter is difficult, largely because at present we lack evidence to judge properly the effect of the relevant factors. As it is, there is no a priori reason to expect the trend of the ratio to reveal a uniform tendency for the recent past. In countries where monetization was extensive, it should not be surprising to find that this factor has dominated the trend of the ratio. This may be the case in at least some of the Southeast Asian countries. In contrast, in countries like the Latin American, where monetization may not have been as important, the dominant role may have been that of the banks. Still another possibility exists: Monetization may not have been as strong in Latin America but its upward pressure on the ratio may have been partly assisted by the effect of inflation; and the combined pressure may have been strong enough to generate an upward trend. Thus, while the tendency of the ratio in Latin America may turn out to be generally downward, we may expect to find a number of cases with upward trend, as well.

In a representative sample of countries in different parts of the world, the pattern is likely to be one of mixed tendencies. It will be recalled, this is essentially the same conclusion of our earlier analysis of the relationship between economic growth and the currency ratio.

Some progress can be made by resort to a piece of evidence. Tables 7 and 8 of Appendix B show that over the recent decade and a half the rate of growth of savings and time deposits has outstripped the rate of growth of demand deposits, as well as the money supply--taken as currency in circulation outside the banks plus private demand deposits--in most of the countries sampled. If we then incorporate savings and time deposits in the definition of money and compute a new currency ratio on that basis, we would expect to find a predominance of cases with downward trend. This is based on the reasonable assumption that the upward tendency of the currency ratio--when the latter is based on the narrow definition of money, no matter how strong it may be, is not likely to be as strong as the upward trend in the share of savings and time deposits in the money supply, recorded in the last column of Table B-7.24

In short, if we differentiate between one currency ratio based on the broader definition of the money supply, and another ratio based on the narrow definition, then, while we may expect the trend pattern of the ratio--however defined--to reveal instances with declining, as well as rising tendencies, we would expect the picture to be more favorable to the hypothesis of declining ratio when we base the ratio on the broader rather than the narrower defi-

nition of money. We shall have occasion to return
to the subject of the phenomenal growth of savings
and time deposits in the underdeveloped countries.
We shall also give an interpretation for the ratios
based on the narrower and broader definition of the
money supply. The use of the latter will also be
mentioned in Appendix A-I.

FOOTNOTES TO CHAPTER FOUR

1. Some of the factors that determine the secular behavior of the ratio may not be associated with growth in the simple unilateral way used in the exposition. This, however, does not affect the essence of the results.

2. Strictly speaking, we correlate with the remainder of income per capita--i.e., after having removed the effect of B from the income per capita, as well.

3. A variable similar in nature to the income per capita--namely, t for time--has frequently been used by economists in multivariate equations to represent shifts in the function introduced by various factors. The latter vary according to the interpretation of the investigator. Dissatisfaction with the results derived by the use of this variable has been growing. The variable has been labeled a "measure of ignorance," and its use is slowly falling into disrepute. Economists are spending increasing efforts in measuring the variables of interest in order to establish meaningfully their effects, rather than trying to identify these effects with some nebulous concepts such as technical progress, etc., represented by the t variable.

4. The use of the share of barter in the total transactions as a gauge of the rate of monetization would not be satisfactory. The shortcoming of this indicator is that it is a relative in which the numerator and the denominator are free to change simultaneously.

5. We do not have adequate evidence on the process of change from production for own use to production for sale. Nutritionists and national income experts would probably agree though that economic growth tends to be associated with change in the pattern of consumption and simultaneous decline in the production for own use. See, for instance, Carlene O'Loughlin, The Pattern of the Fiji Economy: The National Income 1950-53 (Suva, Fiji: Government Press, 1956), p. 17.

6. An attempt to construct an indicator of the size of the non-monetized sector appeared in an unpublished Memorandum prepared by U Tun Wai of the staff

of the International Monetary Fund: "Currency Hoard-
ing and Development Finance," July 3, 1957. Mr. Wai
estimates the share of the non-monetary sector in
the national income by the formula:

$$S = \frac{A}{O} \times V_d$$

Where $\underline{\frac{A}{O}}$ represents the ratio of the number of people
gainfully occupied in agriculture to the total number
of persons gainfully occupied in the country, and
V_d is the ratio of agricultural output consumed do-
mestically to the national income. (Mr. Wai mistakenly
identifies V_d as aggregate value rather than as a
ratio, although he identifies S as a ratio to the
national income.) Using this formula, Mr. Wai com-
putes the size of the non-monetized sector in several
countries; his computations show that the relative
size of the non-monetized sector is larger in the
underdeveloped than in the developed countries.

A procedure such as the one described above is
not valid, and the results it yields are tautological.
For, $\underline{\frac{A}{O}}$ is larger for almost all underdeveloped countries. Hence, almost any variable multiplied by $\frac{A}{O}$
will yield higher results for the underdeveloped than
for the developed countries.

7.   In one instance, for example, estimates of the
production in the non-monetized sector were derived
by first estimating the total maintenance costs of
the prisons in the country; these were then divided
by the total number of prisoners; the derived average
was multiplied by some estimate of the population
living in barter areas--no population census is known
to have been taken earlier for these regions--and
the derived result is used as an estimate of the production in the non-monetized sector.

8.   This is generally the impression one gets from
the literature. On this subject, I have also held
several interviews with experts in the field, including high public officials of foreign countries,
staff members of the IMF, IBRD, and the Federal
Reserve Board.

9.   Obviously, the indigenous banks do not form a homogeneous group, and the nature of ownership within this group is also important. In the last section, the question of the privately versus the publicly owned banks is examined.

10.   Some countries have legislated limitations on the extent of activities of foreign banks. In Ceylon, for instance, the deposits of foreign banks are allowed to expand, but the banks are not permitted to take on additional depositors who had no deposits with these banks prior to a base year.

11.   This is not unusual. In Burma and Thailand, the Chinese minorities predominate in the financial field. In some parts of Africa, minorities of Indian origin predominate. In India, a special caste, in addition to the British, predominates. Historically, the Jews in Europe were the minority that predominated in finance.

12.   An index can be constructed to gauge the significance of these factors. For the nature of ownership, the distribution of ownership by citizenship or by ethnic affiliation may be used as an indicator. For the geographic factor, the distance of the bank --assessed in miles or in minutes of ride or walk-- from the closest bank may be used.   The dispersion of the population in the locality may be provided for by a measurement of the density of the population within a given radius, with the bank taken as a center. The capital of the bank may be used as an indicator of its size. Several appropriate indicators may be used in combination to gauge the standards in business--such as the frequency of forfeits of payments by customers, the average size of the amounts forfeited, the average time it takes to cash a check, etc. Alternatively, these factors can be used as classificatory variables and scaled for regression analysis or tested by the variance analysis.

13.   Looking back at the past, we find a somewhat parallel case in the history of Russian economic development in the late nineteenth century. The short-term nature of the activities of the Russian banks, as well as the low standards of honesty in business, have driven the government into playing the role of industrial bank. This was done, however, through taxation policies. See Alexander S. Gerschenkron, Economic Backwardness in Historical Perspective (Cambridge, Mass.: Belknap Press of Harvard University Press, 1962), pp. 19-20, 22.

14. This suggests that such aversion may extend itself to banks owned and operated by the government; and to that extent, these institutions have an educational role to play. On the whole, however, the obstacles facing state banks are not likely to be as stubborn as those facing a private bank. For, while it is frequently stressed to the individual that his government is interested in his welfare, no such favorable preconception accompanies his approach to a private bank.

15. The relationship that runs through these two channels between inflation and the currency ratio is not purely uni-directional, but rather simultaneous. The rise in prices increases the currency ratio. The rise in the ratio, in turn, exerts a stabilizing influence through the money multiplier. In the case of capital flight discussed below, the rise in the ratio does not have this stabilizing effect, since in that case it (the rise in the ratio) is only a result of the destruction of deposits.

16. To a large extent, this is due to the difficulty of measuring the magnitude of capital flight. The problems of assessment of the magnitude of capital flight are discussed in Paul Host-Madsen, "How Much Capital Flight From Developing Countries," The Fund and Bank Review: Finance and Development, II (March, 1965), pp. 25-33.

17. We do not have direct evidence on this point for the underdeveloped countries. This is, however, the general situation in the developed countries for which data is available, and it seems reasonable to assume this is also the case in the underdeveloped countries, as well. See, for example, the case in the U.S.,--in the Board of Governors of the Federal Reserve System, Federal Reserve Bulletin (July, 1947).

18. Inflation may have an opposite effect. It has been generally held that inflation tends to redistribute income in favor of the wealthier groups of people; and inasmuch as for these groups, the average currency ratio tends to be lower than for the poorer groups, the effect will be a downward pressure on the ratio. There is no conclusive evidence to support the argument that inflation does distribute income in favor of the higher income groups.

19.   The ratios and the nature of the series used in this test are discussed at the introduction to Part II, as well as in the general remarks to Appendix B.

20.   To de-trend the observations, I computed a linear trend for each series and expressed the observations as percentages of the computed trend values.

21.   Simon S. Kuznets, "Economic Growth and Income Inequality," Studies in Economic Development, eds. Bernard Okum and Richard W. Richardson (New York: Holt, Rinehart, and Winston, 1961), pp. 199-219.

22.   Ibid., p. 215.

23.   See the discussion of the statistical aspect to the income distribution in underdeveloped countries, with particular reference to Latin America, by Charles F. Schwatz in Inflation and Growth in Latin America, eds. W. Baer and I. Kerstenetzky (Homewood, Ill.: Richard D. Irwin, Inc., 1964), pp. 258-59.

24.   On the basis of rising ratio of savings and time deposits to demand deposits we cannot say that the trend of the currency ratio will be lower if savings and time deposits are included in the money supply. The rising trend in the currency ratio could remain as strong or become even stronger. On the other hand, an increasing ratio of saving and time deposits to the money supply (defined narrowly) will always imply that when savings and time deposits are added, and a new currency ratio computed, the trend of the new currency ratio will be algebraically smaller than the trend of the ratio based on the narrower definition of the money supply. The trend will be reversed from rising to declining when specific conditions are fulfilled--namely, that the rate of growth of savings and time deposits is large enough not only to equal the rate of growth of currency, but also to more than absorb the slack in the rate of growth of demand deposits.
     To put it in symbols, if the rate of growth of currency in period 2 as compared to period 1 is R_c, the rate of growth of demand deposits during the same period is R_d, the total amount of demand deposits, and savings and time deposits in period 1 are D_1 and T_1, respectively, then the incorporation of savings and time deposits in the definition of the money supply (narrowly defined) will lead to a rever-

sal of the trend of the currency ratio from positive
to negative if the following condition is fulfilled:

$$R_t > R_c + (R_c - R_d) \cdot \frac{D_1}{T_1}$$

where R_t is the rate of growth of savings and time
deposits during the same period.

In the text this condition is expressed more
loosely in terms of the strength of the upward tendency in the ratio of savings and time deposits to
the money supply (defined narrowly) as compared to
the strength of the upward tendency of the currency
ratio, based on narrow definition of money.

PART II

FINDINGS AND CONCLUSIONS

PART II   FINDINGS AND
                 CONCLUSIONS

In the present part we shall attempt a statistical verification of the hypotheses discussed in Part
I. A brief introduction to the statistical material
used in these tests is in order at this point.

The pillars of the study are four ratios computed from data on currency and deposits. They are
termed c_1, c_2, c_3, and c_4. Using

C for Currency in Circulation Outside the Banks,
DD for Demand Deposits held by the private sector,
STD for Savings and Time Deposits held by the pri-
    vate sector,
OE for Demand Deposits held by the Official Enti-
    ties,[1] the above four ratios are:

$$c_1 = \frac{C}{C + DD}$$

$$c_2 = \frac{C}{C + DD + STD}$$

$$c_3 = \frac{C}{C + DD + OE}$$

$$c_4 = \frac{C}{C + DD + STD + OE}$$

The deposits of official entities were included
separately in the definition of the ratio in order
to take care of the not uncommon phenomenon in underdeveloped countries where the activities of several
entities, though official in nature, shade into the
private sector. The broader question of the inclusion of savings and time deposits in the money supply
is dealt with in Appendix A-I.

---

1. C, DD, STD, and OE are all data for the end of
   the year.

The investigation covers thirty-six countries for the postwar period, and nine countries for the last quarter of a century. The countries included are grouped in six geographic areas: Africa, Caribbean and Central America, Europe, Middle East, South America, and Southeast Asia.

For the postwar data, c_1 and c_2 were computed for the thirty-six countries included in the sample. However, available data permitted computations of c_3 and c_4 for fourteen countries only.

For the data that stretch back to the thirties, c_1 is available for the nine countries included in the sample; c_2 is available for three countries only. The nature of the earlier data does not allow a meaningful computation of OE; hence c_3 and c_4 are altogether absent in the longer series.

Further details about the length of the different series and general remarks about their comparability and limitations are given in Appendix A.

For ease of exposition, we shall start with the second hypothesis on the existence of inverse relationship between the level of the ratio and the income per capita, and then go back to the first hypothesis--namely, the recent trends in the ratio.

THE CROSS SECTION

Table II.1 below shows the averages of c_1 and
c_2 for the years 1961-62 in the thirty-six countries
included in the sample. The countries are ranked
by increasing level of the currency ratio. The c_3
and c_4 ratio are not included in this analysis because of the small size of the sample for which the
two ratios were computed.

The table reveals that for both c_1 and c_2 the
European and the South American groups rank lowest
in terms of the level of the currency ratios, while
the Southeast Asian and the Middle Eastern groups
rank highest. The African and the Caribbean-Central
American groups are placed in between these two ends.

Columns A, B, C, and D in Table II.1 give a
modified ranking. In these columns, countries whose
rank is out of line with the ranks of the other members of the group have been excluded. Columns A and
C, on the one hand, and Columns B and D, on the other,
differ in the sense that while the first pair include
Iraq, Jordan, and Syria, but exclude Iran, Israel,
and Lebanon, the second pair exclude the first three
countries and include the last three. This experi-
mentation was performed since half of the countries
in the Middle East group tended to gravitate toward
the lower end of the ranking and the other half toward the higher end of it.

The ranks in Columns A and C are identical.
Both confirm the previous finding--namely, that
Europe and South America rank lowest, the Middle
Eastern and Southeast Asian groups rank highest,
while the Caribbean-Central American and African
groups are placed in between these two ends.

Columns B and D are again almost the same, and
differ only slightly in the position of the South
American and the Middle Eastern groups. Both differ
notably from Columns A and C, in the relative position of the Middle East. The latter improves its

Table **II.1** Rank of the Last Two-Year Averages of c_1 and c_2 [a]

Country	c_1	Rank of c_1	Rank of c_1 in selected countries		c_2	Rank of c_2	Rank of c_2 in selected countries	
			A	B			C	D
Africa								
Ethiopia	76.41	36.	28.	28.	67.44	35.	24.	25.
Ghana	51.00	17.	11.	14.	41.50	23.	13.	16.
Morocco	34.24	7.	-	-	31.77	14.	-	-
South Africa	24.97	1.	-	-	9.28	1.	-	-
Sudan	58.36	22.	16.	19.	50.16	31.	20.	23.
United Arab Republic	59.46	25.	19.	22.	43.99	27.	16.	19.
Average of Rank		18.0	18.5	20.8		21.8	18.3	20.8
Rank of the average rank		3 1/2	4	5		4	4	5
Caribbean and Central America								
Costa Rica	45.66	14.	8.	11.	35.87	18.	11.	14.
Dominican Republic	53.57	20.	14.	17.	43.66	26.	15.	18.
El Salvador	53.33	19.	13.	16.	34.74	17.	10.	13.
Guatemala	59.42	24.	18.	21.	42.01	24.	14.	17.
Honduras	52.90	18.	12.	15.	38.26	20.	12.	15.
Mexico	44.32	13	7.	10.	27.11	8.	7.	7.
Average of Rank		18.0	12.0	15.0		18.8	11.5	14.0
Rank of the average rank		3 1/2	3	4		3	3	4
Europe								
Greece	76.05	35.	-	-	39.41	21.	-	-
Iceland	34.44	8.	3.	5.	11.40	3.	2.	2.
Ireland	26.92	3.	1.	1.	9.92	2.	1.	1.
Portugal	31.36	4.	2.	2.	26.93	7.	6.	6.
Spain	36.44	9.	4.	6.	18.52	4.	3.	3.
Turkey	71.60	32.	-	-	38.00	19.	-	-
Average of Rank		15.2	2.5	3.5		9.3	3.0	3.0
Rank of the average rank		2						

Iran	40.64	11.	–	8.	27.80	9.	–	8.
Iraq	68.23	30.	24.	–	51.94	33.	22.	–
Israel	34.03	6.	–	4.	29.10	12.	–	11.
Jordan	63.47	27.	21.	–	51.12	32.	21.	–
Lebanon	32.28	5.	–	3.	28.74	11.	–	10.
Syria	72.76	34.	27.	–	68.39	36.	25.	–
Average of Rank		18.8	24.0	5.0		22.2	22.7	9.7
Rank of the average rank		5	6	2		5	6	3
South America								
Argentina	60.43	26.	20.	23.	43.53	25.	–	–
Brazil	26.60	2.	–	–	25.78	5.	4.	4.
Chile	41.01	12.	6.	9.	26.68	6.	5.	5.
Colombia	36.62	10.	5.	7.	28.42	10.	8.	9.
Ecuador	49.28	16.	10.	13.	40.22	22.	–	–
Peru	48.50	15.	9.	12.	30.04	13.	9.	12.
Average of Rank		13.5	10.0	12.8		13.5	6.5	7.5
Rank of the average rank		1	2	3		2	2	2
Southeast Asia								
Burma	69.82	31.	25.	26.	62.59	34.	23.	24.
Ceylon	54.03	21.	15.	18.	33.42	16.	–	–
India	72.64	33.	26.	27.	47.68	29.	18.	21.
Pakistan	64.39	29.	23.	25.	48.89	30.	19.	22.
Philippines	63.76	28.	22.	24.	32.62	15.	–	–
Thailand	59.01	23.	17.	20.	44.06	28.	17.	20.
Average Rank		27.5	21.3	23.3		25.3	19.3	21.8
Rank of the average rank		6	5	6		6	5	6

a/ For Ethiopia, Iraq, and Spain, the averages are for the years 1960 and 1961. For the rest of the countries the averages are for the years 1961 and 1962.

position to the second and the third place by the c_1 and c_2 ratios, respectively.

In general, the results revealed by Columns A and C are more meaningful for comparative purposes than the results revealed by Columns B and D. This is so because the institutional set-up in the Middle Eastern countries included in the first two columns is more representative of the set-up in most of the countries in that region.

To sum up the picture conveyed by Table II.I: In terms of the level of the ratio, the European and South American groups rank the lowest; the Southeast Asian and the Middle Eastern groups rank highest; and the African and Caribbean-Central American groups rank in between these two ends--with the Caribbean-Central American group ranking somewhat ahead of the African group.

The distribution of the level of the c_1 and c_2 ratio for the thirty-six countries included in the sample is plotted in terms of frequency densities in Chart II.1.

The chart reveals that for c_1, the modal group includes ten countries, and falls in the range 50-60 per cent. For c_2, the modal group includes three quarters of the sample and falls in the range 20-50 per cent.

This brings up the question of the relative dispersion of the two ratios. A look at the two charts for the range of each reveals that c_1 is more scattered than c_2--even though c_1 is stretched over a shorter interval.[1] The wide dispersion of c_1 reflects partly differences in the evolutionary pattern of the financial institutions among the countries in the sample. When these differences were accounted for by lumping all deposits together, including those of savings institutions, the result has been a reduction of the differences in the level of the ratio among these countries. This result may indicate that the development of savings institutions came at the expense of banks. But this is not the only possibility, nor is it necessarily the general case. It is conceivable that the currency that found its way to the savings institutions would have been retained by the public had these institutions not been in existence. Indeed, given the historic

Chart II.1 Frequency Densities of Recent Two-Year Averages of c_1 and c_2 in Thirty-Six Countries

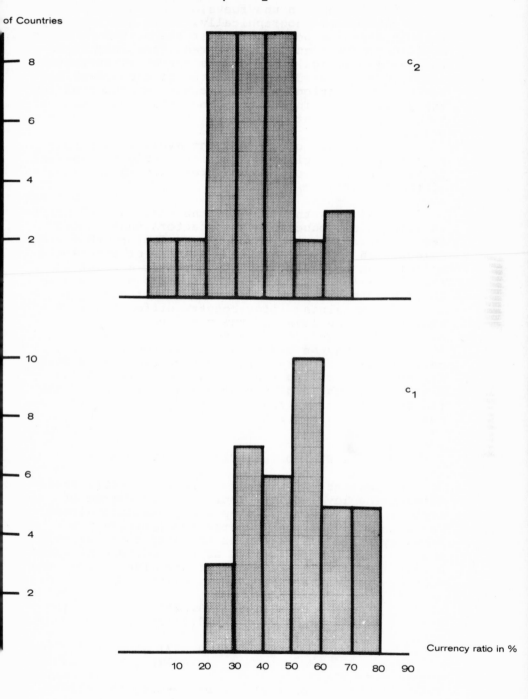

tendency of banks in underdeveloped countries to crowd themselves geographically, it is not unlikely that in many, or perhaps in most cases, the c_1 ratio would not have been much different from what it is today--had savings institutions not grown as they did. In other words, the impetus to the growth of savings institutions may have caused a reduction in the public's holdings of currency that would not have taken place otherwise.

What factors other than the evolutionary pattern of the financial institutions would be relevant in explaining the observed differences in the levels of the ratio?

Inasmuch as the level of the ratio at any point in time is a product of those factors that shaped its historic behavior, many of the factors that are relevant in explaining its behavior over time would be relevant in explaining its level at a point in time. And to that extent, the factors discussed in the preceding chapter would be relevant here, as well, in explaining inter-country differences. Further, since the level of the ratio used in our sample is an average, even though only a two-year average, it may be reasonable to assume that in general short-term factors may not have been significant in generating the observed differences, but that much of these differences are a product of the factors that shaped the historic behavior of the ratio over the long run.

THE LEVEL AND THE STAGE OF DEVELOPMENT

To test the hypothesis of inverse relationship between the level of the ratio and the degree of economic development, a simple regression analysis was attempted for thirty-three countries.[2] The currency ratio was set up as the dependent variable and the real GNP per capita as the independent variable.[3] The results of the test are given below; the scatter diagrams are plotted in Chart II.2.

$$c_1 = 61.67 - \underset{(0.0123)}{0.0259} \, Y$$

$$c_2 = 48.06 - \underset{(0.0099)}{0.0271} \, Y$$

where Y stands for real GNP per capita in dollars.

The results for c_1 are not particularly satisfactory. The coefficient that relates c_1 to the per capita income is about twice the size of its standard error. With the data used here involving conversions from national denominations into dollars, and with the national income statistics for underdeveloped countries being hardly reliable as it is, the results of this test cannot be taken as significant.

Looking at the scatter, it is evident that the fit of the regression line is poor. When Greece, Argentina, and Israel are excluded, the scatter of the remaining countries looks more rectangular than diagonal. A curve fitted by the eye to the remaining countries tends to have a steep slope. The fit remains unsatisfactory, however, in view of the rectangular nature of the scatter for the remaining countries.[4]

For c_2, the results of the regression yield a similar regression coefficient. Qualitatively, however, the coefficient is superior to its counterpart for the c_1 ratio, as evidenced by the smaller size of its standard error. This is also reflected in the more clustered scatter.

Here again, as in the case where we examined the distribution of the level of the ratio, adjustment for the differences in the pattern of the financial institutions in the different countries has the effect of reducing the inter-country differences.

Better results were derived from double logarithmic functions, relating each ratio separately to the income variable. The results are as follows:

$$\text{Log } c_1 = 5.36 - 0.252 \text{ log } Y$$
$$(0.088)$$

$$\text{Log } c_2 = 5.51 - 0.334 \text{ log } Y$$
$$(0.084)$$

In both cases, the coefficients are larger multiples of their standard errors than the linear counterparts. In a way, this is not unexpected, since the use of logarithms compresses the variables. To the extent, however, that a measure of inverse relationship does indeed exist between the level of

Chart II.2 Scatter Diagrams of C_1 and C_2, and the Real GNP per Capita in Thirty—three Countries, 1961.

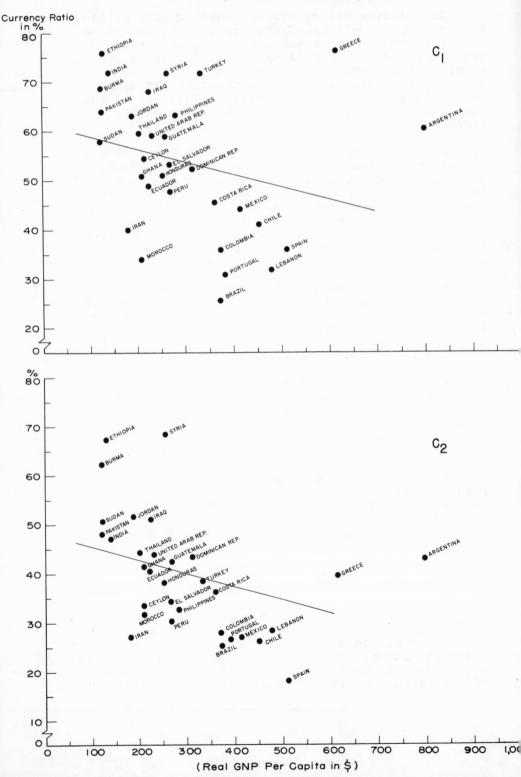

the ratio and the level of development, the double
logarithmic expression has real advantages over the
linear expression, in the sense that it provides
closer approximation to what one may logically expect the nature of the relationship to be.

REMARK ON THE PROPER RATIO OF OBSERVATION

In view of the differences in the extent of
the relationship between the income variable and
the two ratios, c_1 and c_2, the question arises as
to which of the two ratios should form a basis for
conclusion.

The answer depends on the specific purpose
the investigation is meant to serve. When the currency ratio is taken as an indicator of the demand
for currency, the appropriate ratio to use is the
c_2 ratio; for then the question is a comprehensive
one, and the interest centers on unveiling the preference of the public for currency vis-a-vis deposits.[5] From the policy point of view, and in terms
of the effect of changes in the public's holdings of
currency on the money multiplier, the flow of currency to savings and time deposits is important in
the same sense as the flow of currency to demand
deposits. Under the circumstances, the ratio which
incorporates the effect of demand, savings, and
time deposits would be the more appropriate one to
investigate.

When the currency ratio is used, however, as
an indicator of the habit of using checks in payment, the c_1 ratio would be the more appropriate
choice.[6] It must be emphasized, though, that the
information conveyed by this ratio should be interpreted in a relative sense only.

CONCLUSION

The cross section data reveal a measure of
negative correlation between the level of the ratio
and the income per capita. The relationship is
weaker for the c_1 than for the c_2 ratio; but, in
general, the results do not contradict the hypothesis of an inverse relationship between the level
of the ratio and the degree of economic development.

As a group, and from the point of view of the
potential multiplier effect, underdeveloped coun-

tries have an edge over the developed countries, as indicated in the introductory chapter, because of the higher level of the ratio. The results of the present chapter take us one step further to indicate that within the underdeveloped group, a similar relationship tends to exist. The less developed countries in the group tend to have potentially lower multipliers than the more advanced ones. And in general then, the ability of a country in the group to compensate for shortages in development funds-- by way of expanding the central bank's monetary liability--appears to be inversely related to its stage of development: the less developed it is, the better it is placed to do so.

When this method of accelerating growth was discussed earlier, we noted that the ability to resort to this method is modified by the trend, as well as the variability of the ratio. To anticipate coming results, the ability of the underdeveloped countries to accelerate growth by resort to this method has been generally trimmed down on account of the trend of the ratio, as well as its short-term variability over the recent past. It is interesting though that neither limitations--those introduced by the recent trend, as well as by the variability--seem to have been related in any systematic way to the potential level of the multiplier, low or high.[7]

We may ask how to interpret our findings in a long-run context. The answer depends on the purpose of the question, and, therefore, on the ratio we have in mind.

If we are interested in the c_1 ratio, then given the nature of our data, our findings should be interpreted in a very broad sense only--as a rule of thumb, so to speak. Accordingly, we may state that, in a broad sense, there has been a long-run tendency for economic growth to increase the relative significance of the use of checks in payment vis-a-vis currency.

If, on the other hand, we have in mind the c_2 ratio, and hence the demand for currency vis-a-vis deposits, then, while our statistical results are more significant for this ratio than for the c_1 ratio, our interpretation cannot be that much firmer. This is so because the recent phenomenal growth of savings and time deposits in most underdeveloped countries is partly the result of aggressive efforts --in many instances exceptionally so--to mobilize funds for financing large scale development. Accordingly, various schemes for saving, as well as the establishment of savings institutions have been encouraged; and frequently steps in that direction were taken directly by the governments. One may reasonably argue that efforts to mobilize funds to accelerate growth is a consequence of the growth process itself: The change associated with economic growth stretches the horizons, reveals new avenues, and increases the appetite for further growth. This is true. But growth-consciousness as evident presently in most underdeveloped countries can hardly be all lumped as simply a product of economic growth itself. Much of it is associated with the demonstration effect of the military occupation of the war period, increased communications, student travel, and the achievement of political independence. Accordingly, growth consciousness and its manifestations--including the emphasis on savings institutions to tap funds for development--has been in large measure exogenous to the process of economic growth. And to that extent the existence of an inverse relationship between the c_2 ratio and the income per capita cannot be all credited to the effect of economic growth.

With these qualifications in mind, we may conclude that there has been a long-run tendency for economic growth to reduce the demand for currency vis-a-vis deposits.

FOOTNOTES TO CHAPTER FIVE

1.   This is also evident from an examination of the actual range, as well as measure of the relative dispersion of the two ratios. For c_1, the range is 25.0 per cent to 76.4 per cent; for c_2, it is 9.3 per cent to 68.4 per cent. On the other hand, the coefficient of variation of c_1--that is, the standard deviation of c_1 expressed as percentage of the mean of c_1--is two and a half times the corresponding coefficient for c_2--30 per cent for c_1 as opposed to 12 per cent for c_2.

2.   The tests below are concerned with inter-country rather than inter-regional differences. There is no apparent relationship between the level of development in the six regions and their rank by the level of the ratio.

3.   The real GNP per capita figures are in \$ equivalent. They were taken from P. N. Rosenstein-Rodan, "International Aid for Underdeveloped Countries," Review of Economics and Statistics, XLIII (May, 1961), Table 2-C, pp. 126-27.
     The countries included in this analysis are the same as the ones that appear in Table II.1, except for South Africa, Iceland, and Ireland. For these countries the income variable was not available from the same source. In order to maintain comparability, no attempt was made to fill in estimates derived from a different source for the three missing countries.

4.   Some of the deviations from the computed regression line reveal a pattern. For example, in the c_1 scatter, five out of the six Southeast Asian countries lie above the line, and four of these--namely, Pakistan, Burma, India, and the Philippines--diverge substantially. This may be an indication of the effect of some factor common to countries in this region. In this instance, the effect may have been that of the financial institutions. In the c_2 scatter, India and Pakistan though still above the line are brought closer to it. So is the case with Thailand, while Ceylon and the Philippines fall a distance below the line. Burma, on the other hand, is higher above the line--perhaps still reflecting partly the effect of the wide jump in prices between 1959 and 1960, combined with the effect of extensive monetization.

5.   The word "preference" should be interpreted with caution.   In general usage, the term implies that the public has a choice between currency, on the one hand, and deposits, on the other.   In many instances, however, the choice is not real.   In most underdeveloped countries, vast regions exist with no bank or savings bank in sight.

6.   Some readers may question the use of the c_1 ratio for this purpose, on the ground that demand deposits in some countries may include deposits other than checking deposits--book deposits, for example.   To the best of my knowledge, the demand deposits I used in the computation of the c_1 ratio for the thirty-six countries represent only checking deposits.   Wherever there was doubt about the nature of the demand deposits in a country, I used the files of the IMF to verify the components, or to reconstruct the series so that only checking deposits are included.   Whenever it was not possible to do so, I dropped out the country from the sample.

7.   This result is derived on the basis of separate tests of the relationship between the trend, the variability and the level of the ratio.

NATURE OF THE TREND AND DISTRIBUTION OF
THE RATE OF CHANGE IN THE POSTWAR PERIOD

An exponential trend of the form $Y = AB^t$ was fitted to the four currency ratios computed for the countries included in the sample. The choice of the trend carries no implications of a law or a uniform pattern underlying the behavior of the currency ratio. It was made largely on grounds of simplicity and amenability to subsequent analysis.

Table II.2 gives the frequency distribution of the annual rates of change--henceforth referred to as r--for the four currency ratios in the six geographic areas covered by the sample. Since there were only fourteen countries for which c_3 and c_4 were computed, direct comparisons cannot be made between these two groups and the first two groups without adjusting for the number of countries in each group. Several broad characteristics can still be discerned from the rates computed for c_3 and c_4.

Detailed information on the trend factor in each country is shown in Table 2 of Appendix B at the end of this work. A look at Table II.2 reveals immediately a few distinct features:

1. An almost universal tendency for the c_2 ratio to decline and an over-all average rate of decline three times stronger than the corresponding rate for c_1

2. A mild tendency for the c_1 ratio to rise in the Southeast Asian group taken together.

3. Closeness in the **over-all average of the** trend for c_1 and c_3, on the one hand, and c_2 and c_4, on the other.

Note that the arithmetic averages and the geometric averages for each region yield generally close results. This leads one to believe that no serious distortions could have been introduced in the arithmetic averages by extreme values. In particular,

when the sample is taken as a whole this belief is
reinforced by the fact that the relative skewness
(see below) of the distributions of the rates of
change is generally limited. Hence, the computed
averages can be meaningfully used for deriving conclusions about the trend value of the ratio. We
turn then to a more detailed examination of the
table.

Part A of the table shows that for two-thirds
of the countries included in the sample, r_1--that is,
the annual rate of change of c_1--was negative. Half
of the cases with positive r_1's are contributed
equally by Southeast Asia and South America.[1] For
the thirty-six countries taken together the arithmetic mean is -.75 per cent and the mode is -.49 per
cent.

Part B of Table II.2 reveals that r_2 is positive in three countries only.[2] These results are
in agreement with our expectation that the trend
pattern of the c_2 ratio should reveal predominance
of declining tendencies. For the sample as a whole,
the arithmetic average of r_2 is -2.09 per cent, and
the mode is -1.24 per cent.

Comparison of the average rates by geographic
areas shows that r_2 is invariably smaller than r_1.[3]
This is most evident in Europe, and, in relative
terms, in Southeast Asia.

Comparison of parts A and B with parts C and D
of the table suggests that the addition of demand
deposits of official entities does not change the
picture materially. The picture is rather dominated
by the effect of the addition of savings and time
deposits to the money supply: The averages and the
ranges are very close, and the modal groups are the
same, for r_1 and r_3, as well as for r_2 and r_4.[4]

The results shown in Table II.2 are plotted in
Chart II.3 below. Note a tendency to all four distributions to be skewed to the left. This is reflected in the non-zero value of the measure of
relative skewness and in the sign of the third moment
computed for each of the four distributions. The index of relative kurtosis shows that of all four variables, r_1 departs most from the value of the index
for a normal curve.[5]

Table II.2 Distribution by Geographic Areas of the Annual Rate of Change[a] Computed from c_1, c_2, c_3, and c_4, 1948-1962[b]

A. Annual Rate of Change of c_1

Area \ Range	-7.99 -7.00	-6.99 -6.00	-5.99 -5.00	-4.99 -4.00	-3.99 -3.00	-2.99 -2.00	-1.99 -1.00	-.99 0.00	0.01 1.00	1.01 2.00	2.01 3.00	3.01 4.00	Total	Mean of Annual Rate of Change — Arithmetic	Mean of Annual Rate of Change — Geometric[c]
AFRICA				1		1	1	1		1	1		6	-.71	-.73
CARIBBEAN AND CENTRAL AMERICA						1	3		1	1			6	-.69	-.70
EUROPE				1	1	2	2						6	-1.45	-1.46
MIDDLE EAST				1				3	1	1			6	-1.33	-1.35
SOUTH AMERICA						1		1	2	1	1		6	-.39	-.40
SOUTHEAST ASIA							2	2	2				6	-.06	.05
Total/Average				3	1	5	6	9	6	4	2		36	-.75	-.77

B. Annual Rate of Change of c_2

Area \ Range	-7.99 -7.00	-6.99 -6.00	-5.99 -5.00	-4.99 -4.00	-3.99 -3.00	-2.99 -2.00	-1.99 -1.00	-.99 0.00	0.01 1.00	1.01 2.00	2.01 3.00	3.01 4.00	Total	Mean of Annual Rate of Change — Arithmetic	Mean of Annual Rate of Change — Geometric
AFRICA				1	1		3	1	1				6	-2.03	-2.04
CARIBBEAN AND CENTRAL AMERICA				1	1	2	1		1				6	-2.25	-2.27
EUROPE			1		1	1	2						6	-3.62	-3.64
MIDDLE EAST	1					1	2		1				6	-2.37	-2.39
SOUTH AMERICA						1	2							-.70	-.71

CARIBBEAN AND CENTRAL AMERICA				1	1			-.89	-.90
EUROPE			1			1		-.57	.57
MIDDLE EAST				1	2			-1.06	-1.07
SOUTH AMERICA	1			2	1			-.70	-.71
SOUTHEAST ASIA				1	1			-.15	-.15
Total/Average	2	2	4	3	1		-.64	-.66

D. Annual Rate of Change of c_4

AFRICA	1		1			2		-3.11	-3.13
CARIBBEAN AND CENTRAL AMERICA	1	1	1			3		-2.24	-2.27
EUROPE	1			1		1		-6.98	-6.98
MIDDLE EAST		1			2		-1.96	-1.96
SOUTH AMERICA	1	3		1	4		-.65	-.66
SOUTHEAST ASIA		1		2		-1.84	-1.85
Total/Average	2	3	5	1	14		-2.15	-2.18

a/ The annual rate of change is equal to 100(B-1), where B is derived from the trend equation $Y = AB^X$.

b/ For some countries, the period is shorter. For further information on the length of the period, see the detailed tables on the currency ratios at Appendix B.

c/ The geometric average is derived from the geometric average of the B's. It is equal to 100(Geom.Ave.of B's-1).

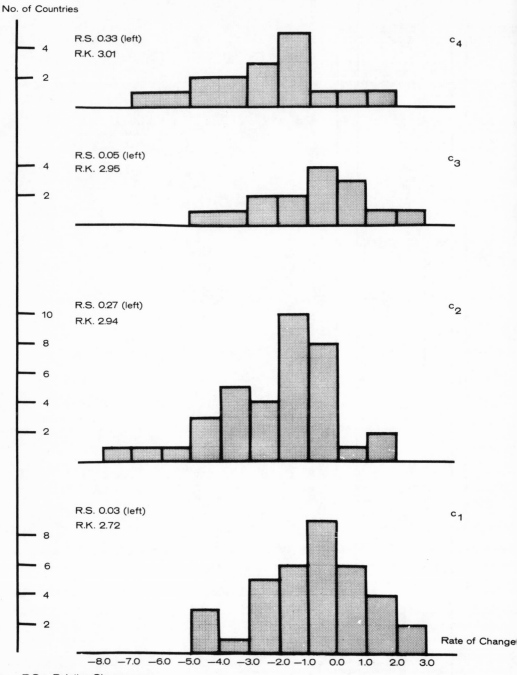

Chart II.3 Frequency Densities of the Annual Rates of Change of the Currency Ratio, 1948 - 1962

No. of Countries

R.S. 0.33 (left)
R.K. 3.01

c_4

R.S. 0.05 (left)
R.K. 2.95

c_3

R.S. 0.27 (left)
R.K. 2.94

c_2

R.S. 0.03 (left)
R.K. 2.72

c_1

Rate of Change

−8.0 −7.0 −6.0 −5.0 −4.0 −3.0 −2.0 −1.0 0.0 1.0 2.0 3.0

R.S. - Relative Skewness
R.K. - Relative Kurtosis

Finally, note the effect that the addition of savings and time deposits to the money supply has on the range, as well as on the relative concentration of the rate of change of the currency ratio: wider range for r_2 and yet heavier concentration on the modal group. The net effect of these two tendencies is a large reduction in the relative dispersion of r_2.[6] As in the cross-sectional case, then, adjustment for differences in the financial set-up reduces the differences in the trend behavior of the ratio.

THE LEVEL OF THE CURRENCY RATIO AND
THE RATE OF CHANGE

An interesting question comes up in the course of examining the rate of change of the ratio in the thirty-six countries: Is there any systematic tendency for the rate of change to be related in any way to the initial level of the ratio?

To be specific, if at the earlier stages of development, the changes associated with economic growth--institutional or otherwise--lean heavily toward the kind that exerts an upward pressure on the ratio while at later stages they lean more toward the kind that exerts a downward pressure on the ratio, then using the level of the ratio as a rough indicator of the stage of development, we should find a direct relationship between the initial level of the ratio and the subsequent rate of change: a stronger downward tendency for the ratio in countries where its level--that is, the ratio's level--is lower, and a milder downward tendency or an upward tendency for the ratio as its level gets progressively higher. A corollary to this hypothesis is that cases with upward trend should generally concentrate on countries with higher ratios to start with. The gap in the cross-sectional level of the ratio among countries should then widen up before it narrows down in future time--if indeed it does.

If, on the other hand, the converse is true, and the changes associated with the earlier stages of development tend in general to lean more heavily than at later stages toward the type that exerts a downward pressure on the ratio, then we would expect to find a negative relationship between the initial level of the ratio and its subsequent rate of change:

The higher the level of the ratio, the stronger
should its downward tendency be; and the lower
the ratio the weaker is its downward tendency or the
stronger is its upward tendency.

A priori, there is no convincing reason why the
currency ratio should go through any set of predeter-
mined or distinct stages, such as rising at first
when the ratio is high and falling down when the ratio is low; or vice versa. Efforts of development
may concentrate at first on the rural areas and then
on the urban areas, or vice versa; alternatively,
they may be geared to both areas roughly equally.
Similarly the financing of growth may proceed in
orderly fashion at first, but then with rising appetite may end up straining the resources of the economy and result in inflation of varying degrees; it
is also possible that the process may start at the
other end. The pattern may further be changed at
any time following sudden or gradual change in government and public opinion. In sum, the pattern of development may vary and with it the behavior of the
ratio.

In order to investigate, however, whether a relationship did exist over the recent past between
the initial level of the ratio and its subsequent
rate of change, an average of c_1 and c_2 for the
first three years was struck, and the Spearman's
rank correlation between this average level and the
rate of change of the ratio in all thirty-six countries was calculated.[7] Then only those countries
whose series begin in 1948--twenty-one in number--
were included in the sample and the rank correlation
was computed for this more limited group as well.

In both of these tests, the results show inverse
relationship between the initial level of the ratio
and the subsequent rate of change; none of these results turned out to be significant.[8]

At a second stage, countries with positive rate
of change were separated from those with negative
rates. Rank correlation between the level of the
ratio and its subsequent rate of change was computed
separately for the twelve countries with positive r_1,
for the remaining twenty-four countries with negative
r_1, and for the thirty-three countries with negative
r_2. The results are mixed, but they are even less
significant than before.[9]

Range charts did not reveal any discernible
pattern either.

As it stands, therefore, the evidence does not
support the assumption that the level of the ratio
goes through discernible stages of one kind or another. Simultaneously, these results do not support
the assumption that there may be some sort of common
equilibrium level, or perhaps a common equilibrium
range toward which the ratio tends to gravitate, in
such a way that the further it is from it the faster
it moves toward it. As it is, countries with rising
trend cover a wide range of ratio levels; and so do
countries with declining trend.

REMARK ON THE RELATIONSHIP WITH GROWTH

Since the behavior of the c_3 and c_4 ratio
turned out to be substantially a reflection of the
behavior of the c_1 and c_2 ratios, respectively, the
analysis may concentrate, without loss of generality,
on c_1 and c_2. With this in mind, could we take the
trend findings for these two ratios as indicative of
the effects of the factors that have been associated
with economic growth during the postwar period?

The period is relatively short. And insofar
as the c_1 ratio is concerned, its trend may have
been influenced in at least some countries by short-
term factors. On the other hand, the postwar period
is unique in the sense that it has been characterized
by a great surge of interest in growth, and accompanied by significant institutional changes charac-
teristic of development. As such the period embodies
the effect of factors associated with growth more
than periods of comparable length would generally do.
Under the circumstances, it would not be unreasonable
to assume that the trend pattern of the c_1 ratio does
reflect substantially the effect of factors associated with economic growth.

For c_2, a qualification has to be made. Not all
of the downward tendency of this ratio could be credited to the effect of economic growth--not even if
we rule out all other short-term effects. Part of
this tendency is exogenous to the process, as ex-
plained earlier. Hence, the pattern of predominantly
downward tendency in the c_2 ratio should be in part
discounted when it comes to assessing the role of

economic growth. The statement is qualitative rather than quantitative, since there is no way of ascertaining what the alternative would have been. It is not inconceivable, though, that if such discount could indeed be effected, the trend pattern of the c_2 ratio would not have been materially different from that of the c_1 ratio--insofar as the generality of cases with downward trend is concerned.

With these observations in mind, the trend results illustrate the point made earlier with respect to the nature of the relationship between growth and the currency ratio--namely, that the effect of economic growth on the trend of the ratio is not necessarily consistent and will differ depending on the period considered.

On this point, the behavior of the c_1 ratio is particularly instructive. As a general tendency the effect of economic growth has been to reduce the level of this ratio. But within the sample, we have cases--one third of the sample--where the relationship is positive[10]--assuming that for the same period some measure of growth did take place in all countries in the sample. The point is confirmed by the results of tests of the correlation between the c_1 ratio and an index of income per capita. These results are recorded in Table 5 of Appendix B below. In general, the period is short--even shorter than the one for which the c_1 ratio series is available, but the results serve adequately their illustrative purpose.[11] Looking at the table we find indication of generally inverse relationship, but with a substantial number of instances with direct relationship between the c_1 ratio and income per capita.[12]

CONCLUSIONS FOR THE POSTWAR OBSERVATIONS

The evidence examined for the postwar period reveals a mixed trend pattern for the various ratios and for the different countries considered. There is, though, a majority of cases with downward trend. These results are not inconsistent with the hypothesis of declining ratio in the countries included in the sample and may be taken to indicate that the net impact of the factors associated with growth during the postwar period has been to depress the ratio in most of the countries sampled. However, these results carry no implications of a law of consistent

relationship between economic growth and the trend
of the ratio.

Using c_1 and c_2 as indicators of the relative
importance of the habit of using checks in payment
and of the demand for currency, respectively, we may
proceed to derive the following specific conclusions.

1.   During the postwar period, the demand for
currency in the countries included in the sample
tended in general to lose ground vis-a-vis the demand for deposits.

2.   During the same period, the habit of using
checks vis-a-vis currency in payment has tended to
gain in significance in the countries included in
the sample.

3.   The rising tendency in the habit of using
checks in payment was neither as general as, nor
was its relative gain as comparable in strength to,
the downward tendency in the public preference for
currency vis-a-vis deposits. This is most evident
in the European group and, in relative terms, in
the Southeast Asian group included in the sample.

4.   The trend of the ratio was not related
systematically one way or the other to the initial
level of the ratio.

The first three conclusions are, strictly
speaking, applicable only to the countries included
in the sample and are confined to the postwar period;
the last one is more comprehensive in nature since
it has been based on tests of significance, but is
also confined to the postwar period. A few questions could then be raised.

1.   Are the tendencies in the c_1 and c_2 ratios,
which the sample reveals, indicative of a generally
downward tendency for the ratio in the underdeveloped
countries as a whole during the postwar period? And
is it valid to generalize from the fact that the
downward tendency of c_2 has been so much more pronounced than the downward tendency of c_1 in the countries included in the sample?

2.   Are the interregional differences in the
trend of c_1 for the six groups included in the sample
indicative of as wide differences among the six continents represented in the sample? Or else could it

be that they have been exaggerated in the sample and should therefore be at least partly discounted? A similar question applies to the results for c_2.

3.   Taking each group included in the sample separately, we find impressive difference in the trend of c_1 vs. the trend of c_2. How valid would it be to assume that within each continent represented in the sample, the differences are as marked as the sample would lead us to believe?

4.   Do the tendencies of the c_1 and c_2 ratios during the postwar period reflect historical tendencies that date back to earlier periods?

Except for this last question, the points raised are confined to the postwar period, and can be handled by inferential methods. This is done in the first section of the next chapter. The last question is historical in nature; and inasmuch as the cross sectional results can be interpreted in a long-run context, we have a partial answer to the question. However, the long run referred to in connection with the cross sectional results does not constitute a clearly defined period. Proper treatment of the subject requires an examination of the data for earlier periods. This is attempted in the second section of the following chapter. Unfortunately, the scarcity of information on the earlier period and the nature of the period for which information is available preclude a firm answer to this question.

FOOTNOTES TO CHAPTER SIX

1. Tests of significance at 5 per cent level indicate that there are twenty-eight r_1's, of which ten are positive and eighteen negative.

   In view of the relatively short length of the period, it should not be surprising to find that generally few factors only, one or two--though different in each country--may have been crucial in determining the trend over the postwar period. In Greece, the rise in the c_1 ratio reflects largely the emphasis put on encouraging savings deposits and on developing savings institutions which have apparently grown largely at the expense of banks. Thus, while c_1 rises slightly, c_2 declines precipitously. The same effect may have been partly in operation in some of the Southeast Asian countries. The indications we have are that here monetization had significant effect; perhaps this was also a prominent factor in Egypt, as well, where substantial efforts were directed toward the agricultural sector. In India, Ceylon, Burma, and Egypt, then, the upward trend of the ratio is likely a reflection of the effect of monetization. In Latin America, as I indicated earlier, although monetization may not have been as significant as in Southeast Asia, its effect might have been bolstered by inflation--particularly in South America--to generate an upward trend in the ratio. In Israel, we have a special case in the sense that the mild rise in the ratio is largely a result of successive short-run effects connected with the spurts in the influx of immigrants and their settlement in remote parts of the desert which banking facilities took time to reach.

2. Dominican Republic, Argentina, and Ceylon. In the Dominican Republic and Ceylon, r_2 is algebraically smaller than r_1. In Argentina r_2 is larger than r_1.

   Tests of significance at 5 per cent level indicate that there are thirty countries with significant r_2's, of which twenty-eight are negative, and two--Argentina and Ceylon--are positive.

3. r_2 was algebraically larger than r_1 in three countries--namely, Ireland, Argentina and Brazil. In Ireland and Brazil, r_2 is negative, in Argentina it is positive. These are the three countries (see Table B-7 below) in which the rate of growth of savings and time deposits was smaller than the rate of growth of the money supply, during the last decade

and a half. At least, in two cases--Argentina and
Brazil--the slack in the growth of savings and time
deposits may well be a reflection of the disruptive
effect of inflation. In 1962, the cost of living in
Brazil and Argentina stood at 610 per cent and 672
per cent of its level in 1953, respectively. (See
any recent issue of International Financial Statistics.)

4. The inadequacies in the recording of deposits
of official entities are discussed in Appendix B
below. It is possible that further refinement on
the data may reveal that these deposits are more
significant than the present evidence suggests, and
that their addition to the money supply does affect
significantly the behavior of the ratio.

5. See Table 2, Appendix B below, for the value of
the moments around the mean.
     In economics, and generally in the social
sciences, non-symmetric distributions tend to be
skewed to the right. The index of relative skewness
of a symmetric distribution is zero. A normal curve
has a relative kurtosis of three. A curve flatter
than the normal--platykurtic--has an index smaller
than three; and vice versa for a curve narrower than
the normal--leptokurtic.
     Tables for the limits of the indices of skew-
ness and kurtosis do not extend as low as thirty-six
observations. Inference from these tables, though
not as meaningful as it would be for larger samples,
shows that for r_1, r_2, and r_3 the skewness is not
significant at ten per cent level of significance;
for r_4, this is not clear at ten per cent, but at
two per cent. The degree of kurtosis of all four
distributions does not depart significantly, at five
per cent level, from that of a normal curve. (See
Eagon S. Pearson, "A Further Development of the Test
of Normality," Biometrics, XXII (July, 1930), p. 248.)
     These tests are based on the assumption that
the sample was drawn at random. This is not true of
the countries included in this study. The choice of
these countries was affected in many cases by consideration of availability of data (see the General
Remarks section of Appendix B). It would be more
correct to restrict the applicability of the conclusion to the "universe of countries with available
data" rather than to the "universe of countries" in
the areas represented in the sample.

6.   The coefficients of variation are: 232 per cent,
96 per cent, 266 per cent, and 100 per cent for r_1,
r_2, r_3 and r_4, respectively.

7.   The advantage of the Spearman's rank correlation is that it is independent of the distribution
of the variables for which it is computed. However,
it is based on the assumption that the sample is
drawn at random from the population. Hence, the
same reservation expressed earlier on the applicability of the tests of significance is relevant here,
as well.

8.   For the thirty-six countries, the rank correlation is -.25 for c_1 and r_1; -.31 for c_2. For the
twnety-one countries in which the series begin in
1948, the coefficient is -.30 for c_1 and r_1; -.37
for c_2 and r_2. None of these coefficients are significant at 5 per cent level.

9.   The results are as follows: For the twelve countries with positive r_1, the coefficient is -.28; for
the remaining twenty-four countries, the coefficient
is .18; for the thirty-three countries with negative
r_2, the coefficient is -.22. All of these results
are insignificant even at 10 per cent level.

10.   Even if we allow for the role of short-term
factors here, the results of rising tendency remain
important. It is also realistic to assume, as well,
that if we allow for the effect of short-term factors, some instances of declining trend will be reversed to rising trend.

11.   Indices of the growth of income per capita are
available for only about two-thirds of the countries
included in the sample. Only in the case of Syria
was the growth of income per capita negative.

12.   No similar tests were performed for the c_2
ratio, since the downward trend of this ratio is
strong and will almost certainly dominate the results of the correlation. I have argued on the
other hand that part of the downward tendency in c_2
should be discounted in assessing the role of economic growth.

INFERENCE: POSTWAR SERIES
THE t TEST, ANALYSIS OF VARIANCE, AND THE q TEST

Three questions were posed at the end of the
last chapter with regard to the applicability of the
findings for the postwar period to the underdeveloped
countries as a whole. This section reports the results of the statistical tests performed to deal with
these questions.[1]

1. To answer the first question, about the
genuineness of the downward tendency of c_1 and c_2
and the extent of the differences in the strength of
this tendency between the two ratios, the t test was
performed. The results indicate that the r_1's, as
well as r_2's, for the thirty-six countries taken as
a whole differ significantly from zero; between the
two rates, however, the results of the test hold with
higher degree of reliability for r_2 than for r_1. The
results further indicate that the two rates differ
significantly from each other.[2] Hence, we conclude
that the r_1 and r_2 results as computed from the
sample represent genuine tendencies for the currency
ratio to decline in the underdeveloped countries
during the postwar period; we also conclude that,
between the two ratios, the tendency of c_2 to decline
is more evident, and substantially outpaces the downward trend of c_1.

2. To answer the second question about the
regional differences in the trend values, the analysis of variance was applied to the six groups of countries included in the sample--once to test if the r_1's
of these groups differ significantly among themselves,
and another time to test if the r_2's of the same
groups differ significantly among themselves.[3] The
results of the test do not indicate that significant
difference is present in either case.[4] In broad terms
these results indicate the following: The observed
differences in the trend values for the six groups
of countries included in the sample exaggerate the
differences in the extent of the downward tendency
of the c_1 (or the c_2) ratio among the continents rep-

resented in the sample. A good part of the observed differences may be attributed to sampling, and hence should be discounted when the results of the sample observations are generalized. In other words, the extent of the downward tendency of c_1 (or c_2) is not likely to vary among the continents by as wide a margin as the sample would lead us to believe.[5]

The results just derived by the analysis of variance are confirmed by a non-parametric test-- namely, the q test.[6]

3. The q test was also used to deal with the third question of the preceding chapter, which was essentially: How seriously should we take the observed differences between r_1 and r_2 for each group included in the sample? Unfortunately, the test did not yield a satisfactory result; and even though the t test indicated that r_1 and r_2 for the thirty-six countries are significantly different, the q test failed to trace this difference to any countries or group of countries.[7]

THE 1936-62 SERIES

The Finding

The fourth point raised at the end of the last chapter poses the question of whether the observed tendencies of c_1 and c_2 during the postwar period reflect historical tendencies that date back to earlier decades. To answer this question one would have to examine earlier series. Unfortunately, we do not have information that dates far back; and even for the World War II period and the years immediately preceding it, the information is scarce.

The series examined in this section are those of nine countries for which c_1 ratio was computed, and of an even smaller number of countries--namely, three--for which the c_2 ratio was computed. Of the nine countries considered, only one is African (Egypt), four are Central American (Costa Rica, El Salvador, Guatemala, and Mexico), and four are South American (Argentina, Brazil, Colombia, and Ecuador). Of the three countries with c_2 ratio, one is Central American (El Salvador) and two are South American (Brazil and Ecuador).

The currency ratio series for the period 1936-62 are presented in Table 1, Appendix C, and plotted in the charts presented in Appendix E.

The prewar period for which the currency ratio is available shows a mixed pattern of behavior. In some countries, the ratio tended to rise; in others it tended to decline. These tendencies, however, are not altogether unambiguous, in view of the relatively short length of the period for which data are available.

During the war, the c_1 ratio displayed a downward tendency. This was the case in Egypt, as well as in Central America and South America--each as a group. In two individual cases, the generalization does not hold--namely, Costa Rica and Brazil.[8] The pattern of decline is not uniform. In some cases the ratio rose or did not change at first and then declined; in others the downward tendency was evident in the first year or two, or even prior to the beginning of the war.[9]

In a few years following the war, the ratio tended to rise in all countries. The slope of this rise tended to be steeper and its duration tended to be longer in Central America as contrasted with South America. In general, however, the rise persisted up until around 1948-49.[10]

The tendencies exhibited by the c_2 ratio are essentially the same as those exhibited by the c_1 ratio for the same stretches of time.

Because the tendency of the currency ratio has been to rise in the period immediately following the war, it is clear that if we had chosen one of the years in the period 1945-47 as the initial year, for some of the countries presently considered the computed trend coefficient for the postwar period would have been algebraically larger than the ones derived in the preceding chapter for these countries.

For the period as a whole, the rate of change of c_1 is negative in seven out of the nine countries,[11] although in algebraic magnitude, the rate of change of the longer c_1 series tends to be larger than the corresponding rate for the shorter series. For c_2, the rate of change is negative in all three countries for which the data are available. It is algebraically smaller than the corresponding rate for c_1 in two countries--namely, Ecuador and El Salvador--and larger in another--namely, Brazil. This is the case in the shorter series, as well, when similar comparisons of the rates of change of c_1 and c_2 are made for the same countries.

Conclusion

Essentially then, the trend pattern of the longer series is similar to the pattern revealed by the shorter series. However, we should not put too much emphasis on these results for the following two reasons:

1.   The sample for which earlier data is available is small and geographically, it is not adequately representative.

2.   The nature of the period of added observations is problematical: Six out of the ten to twelve years added are war years; and the effect of war and its aftermath can hardly be evaluated.

A firmer answer to the fourth question posed at the end of the last chapter will have to await further evidence.

CONCLUDING REMARKS

Two points are interesting to note:

One, it is often held that for the developed countries the convenience of using checks rather than currency in payments was the most important agent behind the decline in the demand for currency. To the extent this was really the case, it provides a contrast to what has happened in the underdeveloped countries. A pooling of the postwar results with the cross-sectional findings indicates that, as a general tendency, economic growth was associated with a decline in the demand for currency. But the mechanism behind this decline was different. In the underdeveloped countries, the decline in the demand for currency is far less a reflection of the convenience of using checks in payment.[12] As a matter of fact, convenience of checks could not have been a consideration for a good deal of the cases.

In part, this difference may be a reflection of
the inefficiency of checking services in underdeveloped countries.[13] More generally, however, the difference in the mechanisms is a reflection of the
fact that the evolutionary pattern of the financial
systems in the underdeveloped countries has not been
an exact replica of the historical pattern known for
most of the developed countries. The departure from
the earlier pattern has been largely dictated by the
urgent need to mobilize funds for financing large-
scale development. The attempts made to encourage
the development of savings institutions in order to
meet that end were noted earlier. And evidently the
phenomenal growth of savings and time deposits in
many underdeveloped countries and the simultaneous
decline in the demand for currency are in part the
consequence of these efforts. More than that: For
that part of the increases in savings and time deposits which is not connected with these efforts, the
emphasis on the development of savings institutions
and the proliferation of these institutions is still
of interest. For, in many instances, the choice
facing the individual in underdeveloped countries is
not between currency and demand deposits, as much as
between currency and savings or time deposits. For
this individual the question of whether or not checks
are more or less convenient than currency in payments
does not enter the picture at all.

The idea may not be far from the hypothesis expounded earlier on the role of the private banks in
the underdeveloped countries, as compared to the historic role of their counterpart in Europe, in bringing down the ratio. In fact, if the indications are
correct that in underdeveloped countries, banks tend
to be generally privately owned, while savings institutions tend to be more semi-publicly or publicly
owned, the above proposition about the effect of the
differences in the evolutionary pattern of the financial system can be recast in terms of the role of
private vs. public and semi-public financial institutions in bringing down the level of the ratio.

A second point of interest is the expansion in
the size of the money multiplier implied in the decline in the demand for currency. The expansion of
the multiplier erodes the ability of the authorities
to accelerate growth appreciably through an expansion
of the central bank's monetary liabilities. Only
relatively smaller investment projects can now be
financed by this method--i.e., if the growth in the

money supply is not to exceed previous limits.[14]
And inasmuch as part of the recent decline in the
demand for currency is attributable to the efforts
of the authorities to tap savings, to that extent
these authorities have been limiting their own ability to enhance growth by resort to an expansion of
the central bank's monetary liabilities to finance
growth. This just underscores the need to ensure
that the flow of savings deposits is indeed directed
to fill in the gap it creates--i.e., channeled to
development projects and not spent for less produc-
tive purposes.

FOOTNOTES TO CHAPTER SEVEN

1. The r_1's and r_2's of the thirty-six countries taken together have been tested for normal distribution and significant difference between their variances. The test of normality yields a chi square value for r_1 which is not significant at 97.5 per cent confidence interval. With the same interval, the Chi square value of r_2 indicates significant departure from normality; most of this difference disappears at 99.5 per cent confidence interval. The F ratio of the variances of r_1 and r_2 is not significant even at 20 per cent level.

Two difficulties remain, which are relevant to the t test, as well as the subsequent analysis of variance. One is that the countries included in the sample were not randomly drawn. Second, each rate of change in any country has a different variance attached to it. An attempt to adjust for these differences failed to improve on the situation. (See the variables that appear under the columns headed $T_{.1}$ and $T_{.2}$ in Table 2 of Appendix B; in particular, notice its measure of relative skewness and kurtosis.)

2. It will be recalled that, for the thirty-six countries, r_1 and r_2 were found to be -.75 per cent and -2.09 per cent, respectively.

The computed t values for r_1 and for r_2 exceed the theoretical t at 2 per cent level--and for r_2 even at 1 per cent level.

The computed t value for the purpose of testing for significant differences between the two rates exceeds the theoretical t at 1 per cent level of significance.

3. Bartlett's test was performed to test for the homogeneity of variance of the six groups included in each case. It yielded an F equal to .4434 and .3025 for r_1 and r_2, respectively. The computed degrees of freedom are 5 and 1157. The theoretical $F_{.95}$ (5,1157)=2.21. Hence none of the computed F is significant at this level.

No test of normality was performed because each cell has only six observations.

4. The computed F's were not significant even at 10 per cent.

5. Note, in passing, the advantages of using inference techniques instead of crude methods for general-
ising the results. Inspection of Table II.2 above
shows that the difference between r_1 and r_2 for the
thirty-six countries taken together is 1.34. The t
test has indicated that this difference is significant. Some of the differences between the r_1's--
or r_2's for the six groups exceed 1.34. Had we
adopted a crude method in the analysis, using the
observed ranges as the criterion, these larger differences may have impressed us more than the difference between r_1 and r_2 for the thirty-six countries.
Yet, the analysis of variance does not show these
differences as significant.

6. This test is based on the use of range as a
measure of dispersion. It was performed at 5 per
cent level of significance in all cases.
      The test presumes that the sample is randomly
drawn. Since this is not the case in the study, the
reservation expressed earlier on this score is applicable to the results of this test, as well.

7. It is possible to substitute a single 6x2 factorial experiment for the separate tests performed
in this section. The shortcoming of this experiment
is that it has to rely more heavily on the non-
parametric q statistic, and the results of this statistic are not always in line with the results derived from tests that use all the information available in the sample.
      The result of a 6x2 factorial experiment is
reported below.

Data For the 6x2 Factorial Experiment

Rate of Change	Africa	Caribbean & Cen. Am,	Europe	Middle East	South Am.	S.E. Asia	Total
r_1	-4.242	-4.156	-8.710	-8.009	-2.321	.345	-27.093
r_2	-12.195	-13.496	-21.721	-14.209	-4.203	-9.372	-75.196
Total	-16.437	-17.652	-30.431	-22.218	-6.524	-9.027	-102.289

Analysis of Variance for
The 6x2 Factorial Experiment

	Sum of Squares	Degrees of Freedom	Mean Squares	F Ratio
Row Means	32.14	1	32.14	$F=\dfrac{32.14}{3.59}=8.9$
Column Means	31.81	5	6.36	
Interaction	5.87	5	1.17	$F=\dfrac{1.17}{3.59}=0.3$
Subtotal	69.82	11		
Within Groups	215.22	60	3.59	
Total	285.04	71		

$$F_{.95}(1,60)=4.00$$
$$F_{.95}(5,60)=2.37$$

These results confirm the results derived by the t test--namely, that r_1 is significantly different from r_2 for the sample as a whole. They also indicate further that no significant interaction is present. A q test applied to each two columns separately for the first row, and similarly for the second row, confirms the previous finding that the differences between the r_1--or r_2 for the six groups, are not significant.

Ideally the q test should also help us trace the significant difference found between r_1 and r_2 to its source, and thus determine to what group or groups it is to be attributed. This can be done generally by contrasting the level of r_1, for each group against the level of r_2 for the same group, and adjusting for the range determined by the theoretical q, the pooled variance, and the number of observations in each cell. As it turns out, however, the q test is not much of a help in this case; not only that, but it also fails to confirm the presence of significant difference between r_1 and r_2 for all the thirty-six countries taken together, as indicated earlier by the t test and presently by the factorial experiment.

8. In Ecuador, when the year 1939 is excluded, the ratio shows a rise rather than a decline, during the war period as a whole.

9.   In the investigation of the behavior of the currency ratio, carried out by the IMF for the period
1937-50, two patterns were generally dominant: One,
in the belligerent and neutral countries of Europe,
the ratio tended to rise during the war to a peak in
about 1944, and decline during the years immediately
following the war; in Latin America and the Middle
East, on the other hand, the pattern was the opposite,
and in general, is in line with the one described in
the text for the Central American and South American
groups. (See, IMF, International Financial Statistics, [September, 1951], pp. iii-vii.)

10.   In Latin America the decline in the currency
ratio during the war period coincides with increased
urbanization during this period. Subsequent rise in
the ratio may reflect the resumption of capital out-
flow to Europe that was halted during the war, the
halt in the urbanization process, and perhaps the
effect of varying measures of monetization and inflation.   Much the same tendencies existed in Egypt during the war period and the immediately following
years. See Philip M. Hauser, ed., Urbanization in
Latin America (New York: Columbia University Press,
1961).

11.   In Argentina and Egypt the trend is upward.   In
these two countries the trend was upward for the
1948-62 period as well, and in the remaining seven
it was downward.

12.   As we have seen, the decline in the currency
ratio was more general and more pronounced in the
c_2 compared to the c_1 ratio.

13.   D. S. Paauw once remarked,"Any foreigner who
has visited Indonesia finds himself tempted to hold
currency rather than demand deposits." The statement
probably holds equally for a few other underdeveloped
countries.   D. S. Paauw, Financing Economic Develop-
ment--The Indonesian Case (The Center for International Studies, Massachusetts Institute of Technology;
Glencoe, Illinois: The Free Press, 1960), p. 146.

14.   If the output is expanding, the previous limits
on the increase in the money supply can be pushed
further. Since, however, the multiplier has been
also increased, the relative weights of the new projects (that can be financed by expanding the central
bank's monetary liabilities)in relation to the
larger output declines.

SHORT-TERM VARIABILITY OF THE RATIO

Since some empirical work has been done on this
aspect of the behavior of the ratio,[1] the work in
this section will be limited. The results of the
tests are presented below without much elaboration.

The measure of variability used is termed the
"efficiency" of the series. It is represented below
by R_4. The index number following the dot indicates
the ratio for which the R_4 was computed. The measure is expressed in percentages. Its nature and
its limitations are discussed in Appendix A-II below.
Essentially, what it does is relate the net change
in the level of the ratio when the last and first
year are compared, with sign attached, to the total
year to year change in the level of the ratio, without regard to sign. What is important to keep in
mind in reading the table below is that smaller absolute value means that the series is less smooth--
i.e., more erratic--and vice versa. Negative sign
indicates that the level of the ratio in the last
year is lower than its level in the first year at
which the series begins. And vice versa for positive
signs.

The Findings

Table II.3 shows the frequency distribution of
the efficiency statistic computed for the four currency ratios. In general, the results do not contradict the hypothesis that in the short run, the
currency ratio tends to be variable, but they indicate that the extent of this variability is smaller
in the series which incorporate savings and time deposits.

For $R_4._1$--that is, the efficiency measure derived from the c_1 ratio--the numerical value is

above 60 per cent in only six countries, and the
average is only 36 per cent. For c_2, the number of
countries with an index exceeding 60 per cent is
double that in $R_{4.1}$ and the average of the numerical value for the sample is 48 per cent. The picture conveyed by $R_{4.3}$ and $R_{4.4}$ essentially approx-
imates that of $R_{4.1}$ and $R_{4.2}$, respectively.

Since the measure is expressed in percentages
and is thus not related formally to the level of
the ratio from which it was derived, one may sus-
pect that greater variability in the series is associated with higher level of the ratio, and should
be therefore partly discounted. Tests of this point,
however, did not indicate that there is any material
relationship between the level of the ratio, on the
one hand, and the extent of its short-term variability, on the other.

The smaller extent of variability in the c_2
ratio is in itself an interesting result. For
inasmuch as savings and time deposits are relatively
significant in the underdeveloped countries, it is
the c_2 rather than the c_1 ratio that is the more
important in determining the multiplier effect of
variations in the ratio. And in view of the more
limited nature of the variability of the c_2 ratio,
it is tempting to conclude that the multiplier effect is not likely to be serious. This, however,
abstracts from the level of the reserve ratio for
savings and time deposits, which is typically lower
than the level of the reserve ratio for demand deposits. Adjustment for the differences in the reserve
ratio may, not surprisingly, show that the multiplier
effect of variations in the c_2 ratio is as significant as, or even more significant than the multiplier
effect of the more erratic c_1 ratio. This underscores the difficulties mentioned earlier in connection with the attempts to accelerate growth by way
of expanding the central banks' monetary liabilities.
Underdeveloped countries may be in an advantageous
position because of the relatively high level of the
ratio; at the same time, the inflationary risk inhe-
rent in the variability of the ratio makes the advantages questionable.

Inferential tests of differences in the variability of the two ratios, as well as the differences in
interregional variability were not possible. The frequency distributions of Table II.3 below do not ful-

Table II.3 Distribution of the Efficiency Statistic, $R_{4..}$ [a/], Computed From c_1, c_2, c_3, and c_4 [b/], 1948-1962 [c/]

A. $R_{4.1}$

Area \ Range	-100.0--80.0	-79.9--60.0	-59.9--40.0	-39.9--20.0	-19.9-0.0	0.1-20.0	20.1-40.0	40.1-60.0	Total	Arithmetic Mean	Geometric Mean [d/]	Arithmetic Mean of the Absolute Value of the Index
AFRICA	1		1	1	1			2	6	-15.27	24.12	44.83
CARIBBEAN AND CENTRAL AMERICA		2		2			2		6	-20.21	35.10	38.31
EUROPE		1	1	2			2		6	-24.08	28.25	32.90
MIDDLE EAST			1	1		3		1	6	-14.95	15.18	22.93
SOUTH AMERICA		1	1	2	1		1		6	-8.24	42.79	44.73
SOUTHEAST ASIA		1	1		1	1	2		6	-2.27	25.12	31.47
Total/Average	1	5	5	8	3	4	7	3	36	-14.17	27.03	35.86

B. $R_{4.2}$

Area \ Range	-100.0--80.0	-79.9--60.0	-59.9--40.0	-39.9--20.0	-19.9-0.0	0.1-20.0	20.1-40.0	40.1-60.0	Total	Arithmetic Mean	Geometric Mean [d/]	Arithmetic Mean of the Absolute Value of the Index
AFRICA	1		1	2	1	1			6	-37.26	30.64	39.83
CARIBBEAN AND CENTRAL AMERICA	1	2	1	1	1				6	-45.08	43.88	55.89
EUROPE	2	2	2						6	-63.67	55.80	63.67
MIDDLE EAST		1		2	1	1	1		6	-33.23	22.00	36.29
SOUTH AMERICA	2	1		1	1			1	6	-20.32	30.51	35.78
SOUTHEAST ASIA		1		3	1		1		6	-43.51	33.12	52.73
Total/Average	6	7	4	9	5	2	2	1	36	-40.51	34.44	47.36

Region						n			
AFRICA			1			2	-7.15	50.38	50.89
CARIBBEAN AND CENTRAL AMERICA	2			1		3	-34.19	46.79	50.97
EUROPE			1			1	29.25	29.25	29.25
MIDDLE EAST	1	2	1			2	-11.20	9.76	11.20
SOUTH AMERICA	1	1	1	1		4	-16.56	30.50	42.50
SOUTHEAST ASIA	1	1		1		2	-1.67	5.68	5.92
Total/Average	3	2	4	2	2	14	-12.83	23.93	34.87

D. $R_{4.4}$

Region						n			
AFRICA	2	1		1		2	-45.67	42.33	45.67
CARIBBEAN AND CENTRAL AMERICA	1	1			1	3	-50.00	62.26	70.08
EUROPE			1			1	-100.00	100.00	100.00
MIDDLE EAST	2			1		2	-29.16	28.47	29.16
SOUTH AMERICA	1	1		1	1	4	-23.29	45.39	48.05
SOUTHEAST ASIA	1	1		1		2	-42.80	41.25	42.80
Total/Average	3	2	1	2	5	14	-41.32	46.95	52.69

a/ The index number following the dot in R_4 stands for the currency ratio to which the statistic relates.
b/ For the method of derivation, see the text.
c/ For some countries, the period is shorter. For further information on the length of the period, see table 1, Appendix B.
d/ The geometric mean is computed from the numerical value of the statistic.

fill, not even remotely, the prerequisites for such tests.

Efficiency measure computed for the longer series reveals a tendency for these series to be less variable than the shorter series in the countries for which earlier data were compiled. The findings are shown in Table 2 of Appendix C. However, these results were not confirmed by the results of another measure not reported here--the average duration of run computed for the same series.

RELATIONSHIP WITH VELOCITY

The Findings

The results of correlation tests performed on the fluctuations in time series of currency ratio and income velocity of money are reported in Table II.4 below.[2] There are nineteen countries; in most cases the period covered is eleven years long. Two concepts of income velocity of money were used:

$$v_1 = \frac{GNP}{C + DD}$$

$$v_2 = \frac{C}{C + DD + STD}$$

In general, the results of the tests do not contradict the hypothesis on the relationship between the currency ratio and the transactions velocity of money. In sixteen out of nineteen countries, the correlation coefficient of c_1 and v_1 is positive, and in two cases it is negative. For c_2 and v_2, there are eighteen such cases with positive coefficients, and one with a negative coefficient. The t value exceeds 2 in nine cases for both tests. This is about half the cases with positive correlation in each test.

The fact that in a simple correlation test such as this, the results turned out to be predominantly positive is consistent with the hypothesis that the spread between the "a" and "i" proportions in the underdeveloped countries is generally not small for most countries. On the other hand, a comparison of the t values for both tests indicates that, while in general t was larger for the correlation of c_2 with

Table II.4

Correlation Results for the De-trended Series
and Income Velocity of Money[a]

| Country | Period | Correlation of c_1 with v_1 | | Correlation of c_2 with v_2 | |
		Coeffi-cient	t value	Coeffi-cient	t value
AFRICA					
Ghana	1955-62	.72	2.54	.50	1.40
South Africa	1952-62	.92	6.85	.61	2.34
CARIBBEAN AND CENTRAL AMERICA					
Costa Rica	1952-62	-.26	-.80	.07	.21
Dominican Republic	1952-62	.56	2.03	.91	6.76
Guatemala	1952-62	.59	2.22	.48	1.64
Honduras	1952-62	.05	0.16	.21	0.65
Mexico	1952-62	.66	2.63	.86	5.01
EUROPE					
Greece	1953-62	.52	1.71	.92	6.82
Iceland	1952-62	.76	3.55	.18	0.53
Portugal	1952-61	.89	5.54	.86	4.74
Turkey	1952-62	.04	0.13	.33	1.04
MIDDLE EAST					
Israel	1952-62	.48	1.62	.18	0.54
SOUTH AMERICA					
Brazil	1950-61	.86	5.19	.89	6.02
Chile	1952-62	.00	.00	.81	4.21
Peru	1952-62	.38	1.22	.35	1.11
SOUTHEAST ASIA					
Burma	1952-62	.79	3.90	.92	7.29
Ceylon	1952-62	.53	1.84	.27	0.83
Philippines	1952-62	.43	1.43	.57	2.09
Thailand	1952-62	-.31	-1.04	-.17	-0.51

a. $v_1 = \dfrac{GNP}{C + DD}$

$v_2 = \dfrac{GNP}{C + DD + STD}$

GNP figures were derived from various issues of the
Yearbook of National Accounts Statistics.

v_2 than for the correlation of c_1 with v_1, the generality of this result is limited. This may indicate that the division between demand deposits and savings and time deposits does not coincide as closely as one would expect with the division between active and idle balances. In turn, this may reflect the fact that the choice facing the individual as to the type of deposits is generally limited.   Probably this is true in particular for savings deposits. As noted earlier, in many areas only savings institutions may be in existence--for example, postal savings--and savings deposits would be the only alternative to currency--regardless of whether the individual treats his balances as active or idle.

The t value for the negative correlation results is generally small: For c_1 and v_1, the multiples are 0.8 and 1.04; for c_2 and v_2 the multiple is 0.5. While the t value cannot be given the same interpretation as in the case of random observations, it is still indicative of the extent of the relationship. As it is, the computed t does not indicate that any of the results with negative correlation are large enough to be material.

In spite of that it remains interesting to look into the reasons why in some instances, the coefficient turned out to be negative in the first place.

There are several possibilities, none of which are mutually exclusive. There is first the possibility that in these instances the "a" and "i" proportions were close to each other to begin with; variations in these proportions associated with shifts from one balance to another, even though minimal, can easily result in a negative correlation, particularly since the series are only eleven years long. Further, to the extent that savings deposits represent in general idle balances, even though part of them may represent also active balances, exclusion of these deposits from the definition of money weakens the relationship and could introduce negative rather than positive correlation results or accentuate the negative results. This must have been the case in these instances. In Thailand, the algebraic value of the coefficient, as well as its computed t is larger--though still negative--for the correlation of c_2 with v_2 than for the correlation of c_1 with v_1; and in Costa Rica, the sign is negative for the correlation of c_1 with v_1, but positive for the correlation of c_2 with v_2.

Another possibility is that the relationship between V_T and V_y may not have been a stable one during the period considered. Coupled with "a" and "i" close in level to each other, small divergence between the transactions and income velocity could result in a negative coefficient. But there is also the possible effect of errors of measurement in the computed velocities. The GNP figures include some estimates of production for barter and production for own use. The computed velocity is then larger than the true velocity. This poses difficulties particularly in the determination of trend of the income velocity of money. A reduction in the share of this non-monetized production in the GNP will yield a declining trend in the measured velocity-- assuming the money supply has increased while prices remained constant--and yet the actual velocity may indeed have declined, or risen or remained unchanged in the meantime. Similar cases could be worked out for instances when the money supply remains constant or declines. The point is that the trend of the measured velocity is no reliable indicator of the trend of the true velocity.[3] Removal of linear trend from the measured velocity used in the tests --and for that matter any type of trend--could not be expected to remove uniformly the distortions introduced by the errors of measurement. It is possible that these distortions have contributed to the observed negative correlation results.

Still, one other factor may have contributed to the negative correlation results. The money supply data on which the currency ratio is based are year-end figures. GNP data on the other hand are yearly figures.

In view of the generally heavy reliance of underdeveloped countries on currency, the predominantly positive results of the tests have important policy implications for these countries. I have argued in Part I, that these have bearing on the problem of the compensatory rise in velocity often associated with disinflationary monetary action.

Regulation of the Supply of Currency
to Control the Rise of Velocity in
Disinflationary Periods

The hypothesis just tested implies that, since
a rise in V_T must in general be accompanied with an
increase in c, the destabilizing effect implied by
the rise in V_T must be associated with a stabilizing
effect--namely, a downward pressure on the money supply. This works in favor of the central banker, who
faces the problem of compensatory rise in velocity
in times of restrictive monetary policy. And if we
accept my earlier arguments that for underdeveloped
countries, attempts to hedge against inflation induce shifts in the composition of transactions toward those that require currency for payment, then
the rise in velocity may come to an end sooner than
the assumption of a fixed "a" proportion may indicate.

The question of how long this process may go on,
however, is not only an analytical one, but a practical one of great significance, as well; for, in the
meantime, much harm can be done.

It has been argued that the rise in velocity
should be taken into account by the monetary authorities, just as any other factor, in determining the
timing and the magnitude of the monetary policy action.[4] Whether or not this is an easy task for developed countries is not the issue at this point.
What is important is that, while some underdeveloped
countries have more control over their monetary system than others, in general these countries are not
as well placed as most of the developed countries in
using the conventional tools of monetary policy ef-
fectively. For these countries, the task of dealing
with a rise in velocity by conventional monetary actions is a difficult one.

Regulation of the supply of currency could be
a useful supplement to anti-inflationary monetary
policy for coping with the problem of the compensatory rise in velocity in underdeveloped countries.
Obviously, the case for the measure cannot be made
equally for all countries. There are likely to be
instances, as noted earlier, where the "a" and "i"
are close to each other; for these instances the
measure is ruled out, and for others, the spread between these two parameters determines largely the

potential effectiveness of the measure. Work is currently in progress to devise methods for deriving estimates for these parameters in a large number of
countries; but if the results of the preceding tests
are indicative of the general situation in underdeveloped countries, the spread between the two parameters is likely to be large enough in most instances for the operation of the measure.

Methods can be devised to suit the particular
institutional set-up in individual countries to exe-
cute a program for regulating the supply of currency.
In general, some sort of rationing system may have
to be adopted. Premium could also be paid on deposits made in currency--with the understanding that
commercial banks will have to transfer all such currency deposits to the central bank.

The measure has welfare implications. For if
my earlier argument is correct--namely, that food
products and other essentials are used in hedging
against inflation and that they are generally paid
for in currency--then control of the supply of currency should be instrumental in mitigating the rate
of price rise of these essentials.

There is another by-product. Control of the
supply of currency, specifically the large denominations, may make income tax evasion harder to come by.
To that extent the anti-inflationary effect of the
personal income tax would be enhanced. Two counter
arguments may be made. One is that income tax is
not significant in the tax structure of most of the
underdeveloped countries, and hence the anti-
inflationary effect that would result from a reduction in tax evasion may be significant in only a few
countries. Second, even if we assume this effect is
significant, the tendency is to increase expenditures as revenues increase. Both arguments are realistic. Certainly the tax by-product may be material
in only a limited number of countries. What the
second argument implies, however, is that the authorities do not take their anti-inflationary efforts
seriously enough. But, for that matter, no measure,
not only the regulation of currency, can be effective.

It should not be surprising that the public
may try to find ways to avoid or mitigate the impact
of the measure. Attempts to substitute deposits for
currency in financing transactions normally financed
by currency, or the creation of some kind of extra-

legal currency, or some other devices are not inconceivable. But all these require substantial, sometimes drastic, changes in the institutions. Hopefully none of these changes will have time to go far enough in the period it will normally take a program of stabilization to make a headway. And, in the final analysis, a great deal hinges on whether the anti-inflationary efforts are determined enough or are allowed to drag on.

The measure has limitations. To prevent leakage it may require a slowdown or complete halt in those development projects undertaken in remote areas, which could otherwise have been financed by the issue of currency. Second, shortages in currency may affect adversely the public's confidence in the financial institutions, and could halt the growing trend of savings deposits, which the authorities themselves are trying to encourage.

Conflicts of goals are not uncommon; they are not peculiar to the proposed measure, and for that matter, the same argument could be made against conventional policy actions. The limitations of the measure should be resolved the same way other conflicts are resolved. To put the limitations in perspective, the alternative should be considered. And inasmuch as the alternative is continued inflation, the limitations of the measure should be viewed in light of the potential damage of inflation. The necessity to abandon some development projects temporarily may then be justifiable on the grounds that prolonged inflationary pressures may result in larger losses of growth. The same is true of the confidence in the financial institutions. The harm of inflation may outstrip the adverse effect of the proposed measure.

FOOTNOTES TO CHAPTER EIGHT

1. See Ahrensdorf and Kanesathesan, op. cit.

2. Results derived on the basis of actual observations cannot be accepted as equally conclusive as
the results of the tests below, in view of the influence of the trend. Two series with trends in the
same direction can yield positive correlation results even though their short-term variations are
very different. To avoid the distortive influence
of the trends on the results, a linear trend was removed from each of the series and the observations
were then expressed as percentages of the trend
value. The percentages thus derived for v_1 were
correlated with the percentages derived similarly
for c_1; the same process was repeated for c_2 and v_2.
This method is also superior to the one that uses
time as another explanatory variable in a multivariate equation, since then one or two numerically
large deviations can distort the results. The findings below should be relatively free from such distortions, since by construction the tests use relative rather than absolute deviations.

3. It may seem that for the postwar period this
difficulty in identifying the underlying trend of
velocity can be adequately handled by using a different measure of velocity--namely, the ratio of GNP
to demand deposits--on the assumption that by elimi-
nating currency from the denominator, the new measure
will also eliminate the distortions introduced by increased use of currency generated by monetization.
While this may be the case, the new measure of velocity distorts the picture in a different way. To the
extent that people shift from holding currency to
holding deposits, the denominator--deposits--will
rise, obviously not because people have increased
their money holdings. To that extent the measure
will show a declining velocity when this is not the
case. And to the extent that the shift to deposits
is stronger than the increased use of currency
generated by monetization, the new measure of velocity distorts the picture more than the older one.
Further, because of possible shifts from deposits
to currency during inflationary periods, the new
measure will overstate the rise in velocity in periods
of inflation, while the older measure will not.

4. George Carvey, "Money, Liquid Assets, Velocity
and Monetary Policy," Banca Nazionale del Lavoro
Quarterly Review, XVII (December, 1964), pp. 323-38.

PART III

The subject of the currency ratio occurs frequently in discussions of financial topics in relation to economic development. At present, data on the subject for the underdeveloped countries are virtually nonexistent. Most discussions proceed from one assumption or another inferred from observations on the behavior of the ratio in the developed countries. However, even for the developed countries, empirical work on the subject has been limited.

The purpose of this study is to make available basic information on the currency ratio, to examine the validity of some of the hypotheses about the behavior of the ratio over a wide range of underdeveloped countries, and to explore the possibility of using the ratio as a tool of economic policy. An initial attempt is also made to analyze the effect of selected factors in the recent trend of the ratio.

For the purpose of the investigation, a sample of thirty-six underdeveloped countries was chosen. The countries are grouped in six geographic areas: Africa, Caribbean and Central America, Europe, Middle East, South America, and Southeast Asia. In addition, the time series of the ratio for the last quarter of a century in nine of these countries were examined.

The currency ratio is defined alternatively as follows:

$$c_1 = \frac{\text{Currency in circulation outside the banks}}{\text{Currency in circulation outside the banks + private demand deposits}}$$

$$c_2 = \frac{\text{Currency in circulation outside the banks}}{\text{Currency in circulation outside the banks + private demand deposits + private savings \& time deposits}}$$

$$c_3 = \frac{\text{Currency in circulation outside the banks}}{\text{Currency in circulation outside the banks + private demand deposits + demand deposits of official entities}}$$

$$c_4 = \frac{\text{Currency in circulation outside the banks}}{\begin{array}{l}\text{Currency in circulation outside the banks + pri-}\\\text{vate demand deposits + demand deposits of offi-}\\\text{cial entities + private savings and time deposits}\end{array}}$$

For the postwar period, at least the first two ratios were computed for each one of the thirty-six countries included in the study. In addition, the first ratio appears in all nine series that date back earlier; the second ratio appears in three cases only.

Briefly stated, the following set of hypotheses in relation to the underdeveloped countries were tested:

I.   The currency ratio has tended to decline over the past.

II. The level of the ratio is inversely related to the level of economic development.

III. In the short run, the ratio is variable.

IV. Changes in the transactions velocity of money require accommodating changes in the currency ratio.

I

Analysis of the trend of the ratio for the post-war period revealed a mixed pattern for the various ratios and for the different countries considered. The findings were subjected to inferential analysis. In general, the results do not contradict the hypothesis of a declining ratio.

These findings may be taken to indicate that the net impact of the factors associated with economic growth during the postwar period has been to depress the level of the ratio. However, they do not carry an implication of necessarily consistent relationship between economic growth and the trend of the ratio.

In general, the tendency of the ratio to move in either direction was not related materially to its initial level.

Translating the results of the tests for the postwar period in terms of the demand for currency, on the one hand, and the habit of using checks in payment, on the other, the following conclusions may be drawn:

1.   During the postwar period, the demand for currency in the underdeveloped countries tended to lose ground vis-a-vis deposits--that is, demand deposits, and savings and time deposits. In general, the extent of this tendency did not vary widely among the six continents represented in the study.

2.   The habit of using checks in payment vis-a-vis currency tended to gain in importance in the underdeveloped countries during the postwar period. Here again, the variation in the extent of this tendency among the six continents represented in the sample was not wide.

3.   Between the two--the demand for currency, on the one hand, and the relative significance of the habit of using checks in payment, on the other,-- the downward tendency of the demand for currency is more evident; it substantially outpaced the gain in the relative significance of using checks in payments. It is not entirely clear, though, whether this marked difference in performance can be attributed mainly to one or more continents. Statistical tests failed to trace this difference to any particular source or sources, although in the sample its relative size is largest in the Southeast Asian group.

To the extent that for the developed countries the convenience of using checks in payments was the important vehicle behind the decline in the demand for currency, point three above implies that what has happened in the underdeveloped countries pro- vides a contrast. For the underdeveloped countries, the mechanism behind the decline in the demand for currency is far less a reflection of the convenience of using checks in payments. In effect, convenience of checks could not have been a consideration for a good deal of the cases. The difference in the mecha- nism is a reflection of the fact that the evolution- ary pattern of the financial systems in the under- developed countries had not been an exact replica of the historical pattern known for most of the devel- oped countries. In turn, this is largely a reflec- tion of the urgent need to tap savings for financing large scale development and the emphasis put on the development of savings institutions.

If the limited indications on the existence of parallelism between the nature of ownership and the nature of the institution are correct, the above proposition about the effect of differences in the pattern of evolution of the financial system can be put in terms of the role of private vs. public and semi-public institutions in bringing down the level of the ratio.

4.   The series that stretch back to the war and prewar period yielded an essentially similar trend pattern to the one displayed by the postwar series. Too much emphasis should not be placed on these results, however. The size of the sample for which the postwar series could be compiled is small, and the nature of the appended series is problematical, since it was intercepted by World War II. Firmer conclusion will have to await further evidence.

The use of income per capita as an explanatory variable of the trend of the ratio is critically examined. The discussion suggests that relationships established between this variable and the currency ratio within a context of gross correlation analysis are only formal, in view of the "omnibus" nature of the income per capita variable. As such, they contribute little to our understanding of the determinants of the behavior of the ratio. Within a context of multivariate analysis, on the other hand, relationships established between the currency ratio and the income per capita are necessarily tautological, and may also be misleading. The discussion concludes that energies are better spent in first gathering data on the factors that directly influence the behavior of the ratio, and that tests of relationships should be subsequently attempted in terms of these factors.

An initial attempt is made to analyze the effect of a selected number of factors that may have influenced the recent behavior of the ratio: monetization, banking, inflation, and income distribution. The analysis is exploratory, since the present state of evidence on most of these factors precludes proper statistical assessment of their effects.

II

Cross-section analysis revealed a measure of inverse relationship exists between the level of the ratio and the level of development. The extent of this relationship is weaker for the c_1 than for the c_2 ratio, but in general the results do not contradict the cross-sectional hypothesis.

The results of these tests are interpreted in a long-run context to indicate that as a broad tendency, the long-run effect of the factors associated with economic growth has been to enhance the habit of using checks vis-a-vis currency in payment, and to reduce the public's demand for currency vis-a-vis deposits.

III

Examination of the year-to-year variation in the level of the ratio indicates that the behavior of the ratio in the countries included in the sample has tended to be erratic--more so the c_1 than the c_2 ratio. For reasons connected with the nature of the resulting frequency distribution for the measure of variability used in this study, it was not possible to apply inferential analysis to the results in order to examine their statistical significance.

As they are, however, the findings indicate that the extent of variability is high. This result is not inconsistent with the hypothesis that in the short run the currency ratio is variable.

The money-multiplier effects implied in the test results of the first three hypotheses can be pooled together. Many underdeveloped countries attempt to compensate for the shortage in development funds by financing investment projects through an expansion of the central bank's monetary liabilities. In one respect, underdeveloped countries have an edge over the developed countries in the use of this method: The currency ratio tends to be higher in the former than in the latter. Hence, other things being equal, the potential money multiplier is lower in the underdeveloped than in the developed countries. The cross-sectional results take us one step further to indicate that a similar relationship tends to exist within the underdeveloped countries as a group. The less developed countries in the group are better placed for resort to this method than the more advanced ones.

The short-run high variability of the ratio, on the other hand, introduces a significant element of risk, and detracts from the advantage accorded by the high level of the ratio. The recent downward tendency in the demand for currency has in addition acted to trim down the advantages of an initially high ratio, and thus combines with the variability to reduce further the attractiveness of the method of accelerating growth just mentioned. Within this context, however, it still remains true that the less developed countries in the underdeveloped group are in a comparatively advantageous position. For neither trend nor variability limitations seem to have hit systematically these countries harder than the more advanced ones.

IV

Test of the relationship between the currency ratio and the income velocity of money yielded predominantly positive correlation results. These findings do not contradict the hypothesis of direct relationship between the currency ratio and the transactions velocity of money. The policy implications of these results are significant, in view of the heavy reliance of underdeveloped countries on currency for financing transactions.

Control of the flow of currency in underdeveloped countries to dampen the rise in velocity emerges as a possible measure. In the underdeveloped countries, the measure could be a useful supplement to central banks for dealing with the compensatory rise of velocity often associated with disinflationary monetary action. In a nutshell, the idea is that restrictive monetary policy which relies on controlling the quantity, as well as the composition of the money supply, could be more effective in subduing expenditures than policy action which relies solely on the quantity of money.

The proposed measure may require the introduction of temporary rationing of currency or a system of incentives in order to attract currency to the central bank.

The measure has desirable welfare implications, as well as anti-inflationary by-products of varying degree of significance for different countries. It has limitations, as well. It may require a temporary abandonment of specific development projects; it may also affect adversely the confidence in the financial institutions. However, the costs imposed by the measure should be judged against the alternative and may, not surprisingly, prove to be tolerable.

APPENDIX A

DEPOSITS OTHER THAN DEMAND DEPOSITS AND THEIR INCLU-
SION IN THE MONEY SUPPLY

THE "EFFICIENCY" MEASURE

APPENDIX A

DEPOSITS OTHER THAN DEMAND DEPOSITS AND THEIR INCLUSION IN THE MONEY SUPPLY

Savings Deposits

The question of whether or not to include savings deposits in the money supply is as yet an unsettled question. Customarily, they have been excluded from the money supply--the assumption being that they are not withdrawable without notice and are not transferable without first being converted into currency or checking deposits. No attempt is made here to delve into the entire question. A few remarks, however, are in order.

A distinction should first be drawn between one part of the savings deposits that is subject to notice and the other part which is not. Savings deposits not subject to notice are, for most practical purposes, identical with demand deposits.[1] One may, however, refine even on this division and distinguish between two categories within the savings deposits that are not subject to notice: One is savings deposits not subject to notice proper; another is

---

1. The fact that these deposits have first to be converted into currency before they could be used for payment is not consequential. It is almost universally true that, except for a limited range, checking deposits cannot be used in the underdeveloped countries to pay for transactions before they are converted into currency. Neither does the loss of interest on the deposit constitute a significant reason for rejecting such identity on theoretical or practical grounds. In many countries--and for that matter, developed countries as well--withdrawal of demand deposits involves a loss of interest benefit.

   It should be noted in passing that, wherever data permit it, IFS includes savings deposits with checking facilities in the money supply. In the sample of thirty-six countries used in this study, there are two countries in which such savings deposits are incorporated in the computation of c_1--namely, Iceland and Portugal.

savings deposits that are subject to notice by law
or by bank regulations, except that, in practice,
such notice requirement is not enforced. The latter
category may be treated in a way similar to the way
savings deposits subject to notice, in principle as
well as in practice, are treated. This subdivision
may be meaningful in the sense that in the second
case--namely, the case where savings deposits are
subject to notice in principle, but not in practice
--the requirement of notification can be enforced
without much delay, if need arises. For the part of
savings deposits that are not subject to notice
proper, on the other hand, such regulation might
take time before it can be put into effect and may
meet with difficulty in enforcement.

In general, these distinctions may not be as
justifiable as they appear, and the exclusion of
savings deposits from the definition of the money
supply, on the grounds that such savings are subject
to notice in practice or in principle only, may not
be entirely correct. For even if we assume there is
a legal requirement of notice, so far or henceforth
strictly enforced, methods of by-passing them are
not unknown. It is known, for instance, that when
called upon, most banks grant loans to their customers commensurate to the size of their savings
deposits. Furthermore, when banks are not required
by law to enforce the notification requirement, the
meaningfulness of such distinctions loses further
ground. For, in that case, banks can afford even
less to be unresponsive to their customers' needs.[2]

Analytically speaking, therefore, savings deposits that are not subject to notice proper should
be included in the definition of the money supply.
In addition, there is legitimate reason for including part of the savings deposits that are not subject to notice proper in order to allow for the
possibility of their monetization.

As matters stand, such account could not be
readily made from available statistics. To be sure,
we do know that in some countries savings are withdrawable, subject to some restrictions--such as the

---

2. Of course, the extent to which banks can carry
    out this policy is determined by the reserve
    constraints.

number of withdrawals, as well as the amounts that could be withdrawn within a given period; the minimum size of balances to be maintained; or the time that has to elapse before all the deposit becomes withdrawable without notice. However, there are no readily available estimates of the distribution of these deposits, the proportion that may potentially be withdrawn--based on past experience--the number of accounts held, or any supplementary information needed for the purpose.

Savings and Time Deposits

Interest in deposits other than demand deposits goes further than mere interest in isolating the share of the monetary component of the savings deposits. Generally speaking, the pattern of development of the banking institutions in the underdeveloped countries has not been an exact replica of the historical one known in the developed countries. As indicated in the text, the choice confronting the individual in most cases is not between currency and demand deposits, as much as between currency and savings or time deposits. That is, for many underdeveloped countries, the historical order of: currency, demand deposits, and savings and time deposits is not as prevalent as it was earlier in the developed countries of the West. This fact is of particular significance in comparative analysis, for the results may be largely affected by differences in the institutional set-up. The incorporation of savings and time deposits in the money supply should improve comparability.

In addition to improving comparability among countries, the inclusion of savings and time deposits in the definition of the money supply may add to the consistency of the series within a country. A shift of preference from one kind of deposits to another, which is not associated with a change in the true economic function of the funds involved, may detract significantly from the meaningfulness of the results obtained, if savings and time deposits are excluded.[3]

---

3. Warburton's study of the income velocity of money in the U.S., with the money supply defined one time so as to include and another time so as to exclude time deposits, brings up this point.

Continued on next page

Whether or not large shifts of this nature did take place in some or all of the underdeveloped countries in the past cannot obviously be verified here. However, there seems to be enough in the evidence presented below on the relative significance of savings and time deposits, as well as on their generally high rate of growth in the countries included in the sample to indicate that shifts of this nature could conceivably be involved.

Tables A-1 and A-3 below give the annual rates of growth of the ratio of savings and time deposits to the money supply[4] and the ratio of savings and time deposits to demand deposits, respectively, for the last decade and a half, in the thirty-six countries included in this study. Tables A-2 and A-4 give the averages of these ratios for the last two years.

Table A-1 reveals that in thirty out of the thirty-six countries in the sample, the rate of growth of the ratio of savings and time deposits to the money supply exceeded 2.50 per cent, and in about half of the countries in the sample the rate was over 7.5 per cent. In only three countries-- namely, Ireland, Argentina, and Brazil--was the rate negative. Table A-3 shows that the rate of growth of the ratio of savings and time deposits to demand deposits exceeded 2.5 per cent in more than three-quarters of the countries included in the sample, and was over 7.5 per cent in more than a third of the cases. For six countries--namely, Ghana, Sudan, Iceland, Ireland, Argentina, and Brazil--the rate was negative.

Continued from previous page

Warburton's computations of the velocity for the period 1919-33 which did not take account of time deposits seem to have been greatly affected by factors which influenced the classification of the deposits without changing their use. See, Clark Warburton, "The Secular Trend in Monetary Velocity," The Quarterly Journal of Economics, LXIII (February, 1949), pp. 81-84.

4. Defined as demand deposits held by the private sector plus currency in circulation outside the banks.

Table A-1. Frequency Distribution of the Annual Rate of Growth a/ of the Percentages of Savings and Time Deposits to the Money Supply b/ 1948-1962 c/

Area	-15.0/-10.0	-9.9/-5.0	-4.9/-0.0	0.1/2.5	2.6/5.0	5.1/7.5	7.6/10.0	10.1/15.0	15.0/20.0	20.1/30.0	30.1/50.0	Total
Africa					1	3	1	1				6
Caribbean and Central America				1			3	1			1	6
Europe			1	1	2			1			1	6
Middle East				1	1	1	1	2				6
South America	1		1		2	1			1			6
Southeast Asia					2	1	2		1			6
Total	1		2	3	8	6	7	5	2		2	36

a/ The annual rate of growth is equal to 100(B-1), where B is derived from the trend equation $y = AB^x$.

b/ Defined as currency in circulation outside the banks plus demand deposits held by the private sector.

c/ For some countries, the period is shorter. For further information on the length of the period see Table 1 Appendix B.

Table A-2. Frequency Distribution of the Two-Year Averages of the Ratio of Savings and Time Deposits to the Money Supply a/

Area	Less than 5%	5-10	10-15	16-20	21-25	26-30	31-35	36-40	41-50	51-60	61-70	71-80	81-100	Over 100%	Total
Africa		1	1	1	1		1							1	6
Caribbean and Central America					1	1		1	1	1	1				6
Europe				1									3	2	6
Middle East		1	1	1	1		1	1							6
South America	1				1		2			1	1				6
Southeast Asia			1			1			1	1	1		1		6
Total	1	2	3	3	4	2	4	2	2	3	3		4	3	36

a/ The ratios are expressed in percentages. For 33 countries, the averages are derived from the percentages for 1961 and 1962. For Ethiopia, Spain, and Iraq the averages are for the years 1960 and 1961.

Table A-3. Frequency Distribution of the Annual Rate of Growth a/ of the Percentages of Savings and Time Deposits to Demand Deposits, 1948-1962 b/

Range \ Area	-15.0- -10.0-	-10.1- -0.0-	0.1- 2.5-	2.6- 5.0-	5.1- 7.5-	7.6- 10.0-	10.1- 15.0-	15.1- 20.0-	20.1- 30.0-	30.1- 50.0-	Total
Africa		2			1	2	1				6
Caribbean and Central America				1	2	2				1	6
Europe		2	1	1			1			1	6
Middle East				1	2		3				6
South America	1	1	1	2	1						6
Southeast Asia				1	3		2				6
Total	1	5	2	6	9	4	7			2	36

a/ The annual rate of growth is equal to 100(B-1), where B is derived from the trend equation $y=AB^x$.
b/ For some countries, the period is shorter. For further information on the length of the period see Table 1 Appendix B.

Table A-4. Frequency Distribution of the Two-Year Averages of the Ratio of Savings and Time Deposits to Demand Deposits, 1961-1962 a/.

Range \ Area	Less than 10	11-20	21-30	31-40	41-50	51-60	61-70	71-80	81-100	101-200	Over 200	Total
Africa		1		1	1	1			1		1	6
Caribbean and Central America					2				1	3		6
Europe									1	1	4	6
Middle East		1	2						2	1		6
South America					2				2	2		6
Southeast Asia	1		1	1			1	1			1	6
Total	1	2	3	2	5	1	1	1	7	7	6	36

a/ The ratios are expressed in percentages. For 33 countries the averages are derived from the percentages for the two years 1961 and 1962. For Ethiopia, Spain, and Iraq the averages are for the years 1960 and 1961.

For the relative importance of time and savings deposits in the monetary systems of the underdeveloped countries, Table A-2 shows that the average ratio of savings and time deposits to the money supply has been in the last two years over 25 per cent in about two-thirds of the countries included in the sample and has exceeded 50 per cent in about one-third of them. For the ratio of savings and time deposits to demand deposits, Table A-4 shows that in almost two-thirds of the countries in the sample the average ratio exceeded 50 per cent and in about one-third of the countries the ratio was over 100 per cent.[5]

THE "EFFICIENCY" MEASURE

Purpose and Description of the Measure

The statistic termed here the "efficiency" of the series is developed to serve as an indicator of variability of the series. The term "variable" series is used in the same sense as erratic series. The measure is then alternatively an indicator of the smoothness of the series. Basically, what the measure does is to relate the net change in the level of the currency ratio to the total path travelled during the period considered. This relationship is expressed in the form of a percentage. In construction, the measure is simple to understand.

First, the change in the level of the currency ratio from one year end to another is added up without regard to sign. The total is divided by the number of years in the period minus one, and expressed as percentage of the level of the currency

---

5. The magnitude of these deposits does not lend much support to the hypothesis that the case for excluding "near-money" assets from the definition of the money supply is as clear-cut as some writers hold. See, for instance, Erin E. Tucker-Fleetwood, "The Money Supply in Mature and in Developing Countries," The Irish Banking Review (March, 1961), pp. 16, 21.

ratio at the initial period. The index thus derived is termed R_1. It is an arithmetic average of the absolute change in the level of the currency ratio per annum. In notation:

$$R_1 = \frac{1}{(n-1)c_1} \cdot \sum_{t=2}^{n} \left| c_t - c_{t-1} \right|$$

Second, the net change in the level of the currency ratio, when the last and the initial years are compared, is recorded with sign attached. The computed difference is divided by the number of years in the period minus one, and expressed as percentage of the level of the currency ratio at the initial period. The measure thus derived is termed R_2. It yields an arithmetic average of the actual change in the level of the currency ratio when the last and the initial years are compared. In notation:

$$R_2 = \frac{c_n - c_1}{(n-1)c_1}$$

The last step consists in comparing the values of the two R's thus far computed. For the purpose, the statistic R_2 is expressed as a percentage of the statistic R_1. The measure thus derived is termed R_4, and it is the one that is used as an index of the variability of the series. It is referred to in this study as the "efficiency" measure of the series. In notation:

$$R_4 = \frac{R_2}{R_1} \times 100.[6]$$

Since R_2 preserves the sign and R_1 does not, it follows that when the currency ratio is lower in the last year than in the initial year, the R_4 value will

---

6. Since $R_1 = \dfrac{1}{(n-1)c_1} \cdot \displaystyle\sum_{t=2}^{n} \left| c_t - c_{t-1} \right|$ and

$$R_2 = \frac{c_n - c_1}{(n-1)c_1}$$

it follows that, by cancelling the denominators, R_4 can be expressed as: $\dfrac{\sum_{t=2}^{n} \left| c_t - c_{t-1} \right|}{c_n - c_1}$

Continued on next page

be negative. Positive values of R_4, on the other
hand, indicate that the currency ratio was higher
in the last year than in the initial year.

The attractive feature of the index is that
its value ranges between +100% and -100%. The
longer the movement of the currency ratio persists
in the same direction, the closer is the absolute
value of the index to 100% and the more efficient
is the movement. Conversely, the more the change
in the level of the ratio changes direction, the
closer is the absolute value of the index to zero,
and the less efficient is the movement.7

_____

continued from previous page

> This brings up the essence of the index as
> expressed earlier--namely, a relation of the
> net change in the level of the currency ratio
> to the total path travelled during the period
> considered.
> It is obvious that the index could have
> been derived by using the short-cut definition.
> However, in view of the usefulness of the R_1
> and R_2 measures for general references, I
> decided to compute and tabulate these statis-
> tics in full.

7.   It should be noted that in order for the numerical value of the index to equal 100%, it is not
necessary that the currency ratio should move
along a straight line--upward or downward. All
that is necessary is that the consecutive movements persist in the same direction--that is,
each movement from one year to another should
contribute toward reaching the eventual position
of the ratio. The less interrupted is the movement the less path is "wasted"--and the more
"efficient" is the series. Compare, for instance,
Table 4, Appendix B and the charts in Appendix D
for the c_2 ratio of El Salvador and Greece. In
both countries the R_4's derived from c_2 and c_4
are equal to -100%. It is obvious from the
charts though that in none of these cases the
currency ratio has declined along a straight
line.

Shortcomings of the Index

The two components of the index, namely R_2 and R_1--provide its two sources of weakness.

The R_2 measure is subject to distortions by irregularly high or low values at the initial or the last year. The possibility of such distortions being built in the computed index appears the more probable in the case of the currency ratio series in view of the fact that the series represent year-end figures, and not full-year averages. To the extent that distortions in the value of the index affect different countries differently, the usefulness of the index for inter-country comparisons may be seriously limited.

To check on the possibility that such distortions may have occurred, a new index, similar in nature, though less sensitive to extreme values, was constructed. First, three-year averages for the first and the last three years are struck. Then, instead of comparing the levels of the currency ratios at the last and initial year, the comparison is made between those two averages; the difference in their levels, with signs preserved, is divided by the number of years in the period considered less three,[8] times the average currency ratio for the first three years. The statistic thus derived is termed R_3.

Next, R_3 is related to R_1, as R_2 was related to R_1, and the statistic obtained is termed R_5. The latter index provides an alternative measure of the efficiency of the series. As compared with R_4, the statistic R_5 should be less susceptible to influences of extreme values of the currency ratio in years at either end of the series.[9]

---

8. For each of the two computed averages one degree of freedom is lost. A third degree of freedom is lost in the differencing process.

9. From examination of Table 4, Appendix B, it can be seen that the numerical value of the R_5 index may exceed 100%. This follows from the method of its construction. The index could be adjusted though so that its values range between -100% and +100%.

To compare the two pictures conveyed by the alternative measures, the Spearman's rank correlation was used. The results revealed that for each of the four currency ratios, the numerical value of R_2 correlates highly with that of R_3. Similarly, R_4 and R_5 correlate as highly.[10] In all cases, the coefficients were significant at 1% level of significance.

Thus, the results did not bear out the suspicion that irregularities in the level of the currency ratio at either end of the series may have distorted the value of R_4, or detracted seriously from its usefulness for inter-country comparisons. In view of this finding, only the results of the R_4 measure are summarized in the text.[11]

The second source of weakness in the "efficiency" measure derives from the R_1 component. The latter cannot distinguish between a series with one or two large swings, on the one hand, and another with more frequent, but less pronounced changes in direction on

---

10. The fact that both R_2 and R_3 are divided by the same number--namely, R_1--to obtain R_4 and R_5, respectively, does not necessarily imply that if R_2 correlates highly with R_3, the same thing must be true of R_4 and R_5. To illustrate suppose that for two countries A and B, we have the following picture:

Country	R_1	R_2	R_3	$R_4 = \dfrac{R_2}{R_1}$	$R_5 = \dfrac{R_3}{R_1}$	R_2	Rank R_3	R_4	R_5
A	2	.7	.8	.35	.4	1	1	1	2
B	1	.3	.5	.3	.5	2	2	2	1

It is clear from the table that R_2 and R_3 correlate perfectly. Division by R_1, however, upsets this relationship, as can be seen by examining the ranks of R_4 and R_5.

11. The loss of degrees of freedom dictated by the construction of R_5 is rather significant for series whose length does not exceed fifteen years. This in itself, other things being equal, favors the use of R_4 rather than R_5.

the other. The difficulty stems from the fact that
the index is based solely on the magnitude of change.[12]
In order to test for this possibility an additional
statistic--a modified version of the National Bureau's
Average Duration of Run--was computed, and the results
compared. They did not indicate that the problem that
derives from the R_1 component was of any consequence.

---

12. It is possible to construct--with much difficulty
    and arbitrariness, though--a duration-magnitude
    index which combines the effect of both factors:
    duration and magnitude.

APPENDIX B

DATA FOR THE 1948-62 PERIOD

APPENDIX B

DATA FOR THE 1948-62 PERIOD
SOURCES AND NOTES

Sources

The computations that appear in this appendix
use data on:

1. Currency, demand deposits of the private
sector, savings and time deposits of the private
sector, and demand deposits of official entities,
compiled in part from the files of the International
Monetary Fund, and in part from issues of the International Financial Statistics.

2. U.S. dollar assets held by the private sector and cost of living indices--derived from various
issues of the International Financial Statistics.

3. Income per capita indices derived from
various publications of the United Nation's Statistical Yearbook.

General Remarks on the Data

Availability of data determined in many instances the choice of the countries included in the
sample. The limitation imposed by this factor was
inconsequential for the Latin American, as well as
the Southeast Asian countries. It was particularly
disturbing in the case of the African countries.
Here, in order to maintain a uniform number of countries in each group,[1] it was necessary to include

_____

1. The reasons why samples of equal size for each
   group were preferred are the expected improvement in the estimate of the variance of the difference of two means and in the detection of inequality among means; the necessity for the subsequent q test whose application requires uniform-
   ity of size; and the convenience and simplicity
   of computations based on equal sample size.

Morocco, and South Africa in the sample--the first with series consisting of observations for five years only, and the latter with a peculiar status that hardly permits a classification by level of economic development.

All through, consistency in definition of the different ratio concepts was maintained as much as available data allow. The deposits of official entities present a difficult problem, since some countries report them separately, while others report them as part of the deposits of the government. Furthermore, not all the countries are agreed on what the term official entities should include. Wherever the data permit it, the demand deposits of the private sector were cleared of the deposits of official entities. However, there remain three countries-- namely, Peru, Mexico, and Ghana--where at least part of these deposits remain in the demand deposits of the private sector. In three other countries-- Turkey, Thailand, and Ceylon--it is not certain exactly where and to what extent the official entities' deposits are included. It is suspected that part of these deposits may have been included in the demand deposits of the private sector, as well.[2]

There are other problems of definition, treatment of border line cases, and inclusiveness of reporting which raise questions of comparability among and within the countries.[3]

The lacuna of detailed information for the war and the pre-war period is striking indeed. This has at times necessitated a compromise in the definitions, in order to maintain reasonable consistency within countries for the period considered. As a result, computations of c_1 for the fifties that appear in the longer series may somewhat differ from

---

2. Isolation of the currency held by official entities was not possible to achieve. This means that the c_1 ratios may be overstated in at least some instances.

3. These and other problems are discussed in the Reprints of introductory articles, published in the January to May, 1960 issues of the IFS.

the computations of c_1 for the fifties that appear
in the postwar series for the same country. As I
have pointed out, this is so because adjustments
had to be made in the longer series in order to put
more recent parts of these series on a consistent
basis with the thirties and the early forties.

Table B-1. Currency Ratio [1/] 1948-1962

		1948	1949	1950	1951	1952	1953	1954	1955	1956	1957	1958	1959	1960	1961	1962
AFRICA																
Ethiopia	c_1	77.28	80.15	76.76	83.09	79.79	80.36	83.76	81.29	79.86	77.11	74.65	77.85	75.74	77.07	
	c_2	75.70	76.81	74.04	74.56	74.56	75.64	76.71	74.14	70.64	68.29	67.00	69.68	67.16	67.72	
Ghana	c_1			76.72	77.23	73.18	70.56	67.71	67.50	69.87	66.87	63.44	65.44	64.83	47.32	54.69
	c_2			64.88	65.00	61.69	58.69	56.57	56.20	57.71	53.39	49.38	50.96	51.12	39.42	43.58
Morocco	c_1										35.39	35.92	36.07	34.14	34.34	
	c_2										33.10	34.26	33.22	31.65	31.89	
South Africa	c_1	17.09	18.85	18.74	20.04	21.60	22.42	22.97	24.76	25.01	25.39	26.32	24.49	25.83	25.52	23.63
	c_2	10.40	10.93	10.95	11.57	11.92	12.19	11.76	11.60	11.07	10.64	10.66	9.92	9.54	9.60	8.96
	c_3	16.83	18.43	18.23	19.59	21.12	21.83	22.35	24.12	24.30	24.54	25.48	24.49	24.99	24.52	22.84
	c_4	10.30	10.79	10.77	11.42	11.77	12.02	11.60	11.46	10.93	10.49	10.52	9.78	9.42	9.48	8.85
Sudan	c_1			83.07	85.67	82.20					65.03	62.89	60.06	57.72	58.16	58.55
	c_2			88.82	71.95	75.16					55.17	55.91	53.06	49.56	50.05	50.28
	c_3			88.44	65.98	72.42					51.11	61.15	53.66	51.02	50.32	51.61
	c_4			82.74		66.90								44.54	44.13	45.07
United Arab Republic	c_1			46.69	51.29	51.91	49.37	50.06	48.23	52.09	51.35	52.89	48.33	51.96	57.94	60.97
	c_2			40.47	44.50	44.18	41.01	40.91	39.30	43.68	42.57	41.68	37.27	40.48	45.18	42.80
CARIBBEAN AND CENTRAL AMERICA																
Costa Rica	c_1	62.63	54.72	49.63	51.35	49.56	50.11	51.00	48.65	47.25	48.52	47.77	46.14	46.99	45.67	45.65
	c_2	57.45	49.53	44.36	45.68	43.86	44.02	44.65	41.36	39.65	40.39	38.79	36.90	37.35	35.98	35.76
	c_3	60.43	51.62	47.23	48.31	47.34	47.52	47.77	45.01	44.18	45.73	45.39	43.49	44.74	43.83	43.00
	c_4	55.59	46.98	42.44	42.44	42.00	42.00	42.16	38.70	38.43	37.21	37.15	35.19	35.92	35.81	34.12
Dominican Republic	c_1			36.10	37.80	38.40	41.61	35.31	36.41	53.62	34.19	34.19	35.55	35.92	35.98	34.12
	c_2			43.36	44.68	45.57	50.00	48.52	51.75	51.81	51.16	41.19	42.37	46.67	49.76	44.96
	c_3			35.57	37.18	37.72	41.01	34.85	35.72	34.91	33.77	34.19	35.55	36.97	40.99	53.29
El Salvador	c_1	70.04	67.14	63.89	62.41	61.47	58.02	56.51	51.71	49.48	49.88	48.97	48.93	51.17	40.99	43.61
	c_2	69.30	65.81	62.94	62.41	60.85	57.13	55.51	50.44	49.48	48.97	43.78	41.01	40.05	37.11	52.39
	c_3	67.27	64.05	58.97	57.89	57.23	55.28	54.51	49.62	49.48	47.71	43.78	46.40	48.30	36.01	32.36
	c_4	66.59	62.84	58.16	57.14	56.69	54.48	53.60	48.45	47.07	44.48	42.08	39.22	38.27	43.45	31.45
Guatemala	c_1	66.13	62.84	65.93	66.67	63.46	61.45	63.51	59.48	48.64	47.06	56.58	45.82	60.08	43.45	58.44
	c_2	60.13	61.03	57.63	58.05	55.10	54.80	53.31	55.22	56.41	59.48	56.58	56.46	44.68	43.45	40.57
Honduras	c_1	45.40	50.75	51.61	53.31	55.10	47.70	51.83	53.31	56.41	59.48	57.73	55.46	55.22	53.49	52.30
	c_2	39.48	43.80	46.72	46.72	46.72	41.70	49.40	46.25	48.64	47.06	46.25	45.35	41.35	39.28	37.25
Mexico	c_1	51.50	53.16	47.18	49.98	50.68	48.44	51.83	47.55	48.15	47.98	48.50	45.96	45.65	44.88	44.00
	c_2	41.01	42.45	37.91	38.84	39.37	36.66	36.08	33.75	34.24	34.18	34.66	31.19	29.29	27.88	26.53
EUROPE																
Greece	c_1						73.43	70.24	69.59	75.53	74.63	74.93	74.37	74.56	74.86	77.24
	c_2						70.83	66.04	63.90	60.44	49.79	44.99	41.11	40.79	40.16	38.66
	c_3						67.46	66.15	65.95	71.87	70.53	69.31	69.27	69.29	69.72	70.92
	c_4						65.26	62.42	60.82	58.07	47.93	42.91	39.50	39.13	38.63	37.01
Iceland	c_1				49.24	51.42	57.97	54.18	43.38	45.05	40.49	38.93	35.99	36.68	34.96	33.92
	c_2				19.50	19.46	20.57	17.30	16.96	17.22	15.69	15.31	13.77	12.22	11.80	10.99
Ireland	c_1	33.60	33.53	34.86	33.89	35.74	37.60	30.79	36.13	34.65	35.47	31.45	30.47	29.29	28.15	25.69
	c_2	11.95	11.91	12.47	12.38	13.24	13.81	10.30	13.33	12.72	13.30	11.44	10.75	10.82	10.35	9.50
Portugal	c_1	32.02	33.00	31.70	30.74	30.54	29.62	28.76	29.07	29.60	28.66	28.10	27.70	27.38	27.76	30.83
	c_2	30.88	31.90	30.61	29.70	29.34	28.28	28.76	27.35	27.69	26.64	25.84	25.19	24.29	24.29	26.10
Spain	c_1			44.19	27.76	41.00	38.65	38.29	36.29	36.13	35.85	35.85	35.52	37.09	35.78	9.50
	c_2			28.95		25.38	23.04	28.38	20.70	20.84	21.89	21.13	20.61	19.06	17.97		
Turkey	c_1	80.74	80.74	80.59	77.51	71.58	70.64	67.17	68.35	70.07	72.24	70.45	69.07	70.82	71.03	72.17
	c_2	54.02	54.02	51.00	48.28	44.75	40.67	37.98	39.91	40.11	39.92	39.00	37.38	38.66	38.02	37.99
MIDDLE EAST																
Iran	c_1					54.24	52.78	51.70	48.07	45.19	42.61	36.55	35.71	33.15	40.62	40.66

	c_2															
	c_3															
	c_1	47.50														
	c_2	46.80														
Lebanon	c_2		58.67	63.38	63.19	64.88	61.02	65.47	59.94	60.04	57.95	55.05	53.18	49.07		
	c_3		58.58	61.12	62.73	63.56	63.64	71.90	66.23	62.31	63.02	59.91	58.68	56.89		
	c_1		55.81	57.65	58.64	59.18	58.00	63.92	57.80	54.79	54.17	51.52	49.15	45.59		
	c_2		44.03	45.28	47.10	48.54	45.95	51.04	43.42	46.43	43.59	35.78	33.61	30.95		
Syria	c_1		43.45	45.03	45.03	42.93	74.53	47.83	77.39	74.47	70.83	67.54	72.91	72.60		
	c_2		70.03	78.00	77.05	76.31	74.53	78.54	77.39	74.04	70.83	67.97	72.06	68.24		
	c_3		69.01	78.00	77.05	76.31	74.53	72.06	72.64	72.64	69.31	61.26	65.77	64.80		
	c_4		69.01	76.22	74.73	73.63	71.01	69.02	69.68	66.14	62.63	57.05	62.19	61.30		

SOUTH AMERICA

Argentina	c_1	48.95	51.59	54.01	57.44	60.03	58.48	60.94	60.00	61.66	61.87	59.94	60.04	60.99	59.38	59.23	58.98	59.05	57.95	55.05	53.18	61.63
	c_2	32.25	34.33	37.44	41.20	43.43	42.62	44.18	41.10	45.05	43.45	43.33	42.31	43.33	44.99	43.13	43.92	43.92
	c_3	41.02	44.55	48.18	50.58	53.27	51.17	51.54	50.71	52.02	50.49	50.49	54.17	50.73	49.63	50.06	48.30	54.09
	c_4	28.61	31.06	34.54	35.11	39.78	38.60	39.02	36.51	37.51	36.51	31.40	43.59	31.40	28.34	27.95	37.37	39.96
Brazil	c_1	37.34	34.65	35.30	35.11	33.33	33.45	35.25	34.49	34.84	31.32	31.32	31.40	31.40	28.34	27.53	37.11	25.25
	c_2	30.89	28.68	29.53	29.58	28.71	29.26	31.07	31.48	31.41	28.90	28.90	29.30	28.90	26.87	26.30	26.30	24.56
	c_3	35.40	33.16	32.06	31.35	30.23	30.48	31.07	31.06	32.10	27.95	27.95	28.24	27.95	25.38	24.47	24.55	22.66
	c_4	29.25	27.65	27.22	26.87	26.38	26.96	28.79	28.60	29.16	26.01	26.01	26.52	26.01	24.20	23.49	23.81	22.10
Chile	c_1	34.40	33.12	37.80	40.84	44.71	44.65	42.70	44.27	43.23	44.27	44.27	42.03	42.50	42.46	41.47	40.66	41.36
	c_2	28.67	26.77	28.97	31.20	35.08	35.01	34.34	37.36	36.41	33.93	33.93	33.36	42.03	29.24	28.74	37.37	26.00
	c_3	34.40	33.12	37.14	37.14	39.31	38.13	35.19	37.36	38.00	37.15	37.15	37.15	37.15	27.64	34.60	34.37	32.83
	c_4	28.67	26.77	28.97	31.67	31.67	30.87	29.31	30.67	32.62	31.10	31.10	30.21	31.10	27.64	25.26	24.37	22.35
Colombia	c_1	49.54	53.02	47.89	46.05	46.21	44.06	41.45	41.03	41.03	43.68	43.68	42.17	43.25	41.37	40.72	37.63	35.61
	c_2	39.73	44.43	39.00	36.22	35.22	34.51	30.67	30.77	32.62	33.84	33.84	33.25	33.25	31.70	31.16	29.16	27.68
	c_3	44.62	54.61	52.60	55.10	52.76	52.80	52.29	53.09	52.66	52.66	52.66	52.36	52.66	49.64	49.94	49.91	48.64
	c_4	47.84	50.37	47.71	47.71	45.24	45.24	44.25	43.73	43.00	43.00	43.00	43.00	40.67	40.67	41.19	40.71	39.74
Ecuador	c_1	51.60	52.02	50.37	52.16	49.13	49.13	48.68	49.37	49.38	49.38	49.38	48.40	48.40	46.08	45.85	46.81	46.00
	c_2	45.25	45.65	44.11	45.49	43.15	42.52	41.82	41.63	41.25	41.25	40.28	40.28	40.74	38.24	38.37	38.62	37.96
	c_3	44.28	48.27	48.55	45.49	45.38	45.38	46.32	46.46	47.98	47.98	51.31	50.44	48.51	48.51	46.14	50.87
	c_4	33.43	35.28	34.93	31.68	30.06	30.83	31.12	29.74	30.32	29.48	31.94	33.57	31.14	31.14	29.92	30.15

SOUTHEAST ASIA

Burma	c_1	67.13	64.86	65.68	69.45	66.40	67.34	64.96	61.80	61.45	67.45	65.06	69.21	68.44	69.02	70.62
	c_2	63.69	60.68	61.14	64.90	62.50	61.76	58.61	57.40	57.40	61.86	59.69	60.67	61.52	62.04	63.13
Ceylon	c_1	39.70	36.19	38.04	40.43	40.95	36.11	36.16	35.87	42.15	49.67	48.33	49.71	54.57	53.49
	c_2	28.02	27.79	27.36	28.07	27.82	25.05	25.41	24.62	27.36	31.47	30.43	30.16	33.81	33.04
India	c_1	68.69	69.11	69.98	69.97	70.84	69.68	70.54	70.77	69.82	71.05	72.13	72.32	72.82	72.46
	c_2	58.69	57.28	57.43	57.49	55.77	55.84	54.36	53.70	50.14	47.87	46.42	47.45	47.74	47.63
Pakistan	c_1	64.75	67.94	66.71	67.05	55.95	67.71	68.44	70.40	68.01	66.71	65.60	65.60	63.18
	c_2	55.11	55.33	57.95	57.13	56.65	55.84	56.87	58.75	56.00	53.27	53.96	50.92	46.85
	c_3	63.24	63.25	65.75	66.88	66.55	66.85	68.26	70.29	67.95	65.73	67.83	65.11	61.44
	c_4	54.01	53.45	57.62	57.23	57.01	55.26	56.75	58.67	55.96	56.72	53.94	50.63	45.88
Philippines	c_1	72.36	71.07	65.28	70.85	69.46	71.31	67.81	66.24	62.73	56.72	66.88	64.32	65.24	62.83
	c_2	52.36	51.03	49.85	50.56	49.70	47.91	44.76	42.08	38.90	42.08	37.88	38.58	34.34	30.90
	c_3	54.14	61.03	59.68	58.77	61.10	43.13	57.66	56.67	55.68	38.33	58.51	57.71	56.45	55.49
	c_4			62.28	44.65	44.52	33.33	40.10	42.74	36.07	38.34	35.04	36.11	31.87	29.01
Thailand	c_1	42.11	45.64	46.52	47.60	72.44	68.60	71.65	70.12	65.09	67.93	60.02	63.66	58.77	59.24
	c_2					66.67	62.71	64.11	61.94	55.39	59.07	52.93	48.87	46.49	41.63

a/ Using: C for currency in circulation outside the banks, DD for demand deposits held by the private sector, STD for savings and time deposits held by the private sector, OE for demand deposits held by the official entities, the currency ratios that appear in this table are as follows:

$$c_1 = \frac{C}{C + DD} \qquad c_2 = \frac{C}{C + DD + STD} \qquad c_3 = \frac{C}{C + DD + OE} \qquad c_4 = \frac{C}{C + DD + STD + OE}$$

C, DD, STD, and OE are all data for the end of each year.

Supplement to Table B-1

Africa

		1962	1963	1964
Ethiopia	c_1	76.65	73.95	73.10
	c_2	65.94	62.61	59.61
Ghana	c_1		56.59	55.14
	c_2		43.36	41.55
Morocco	c_1		36.84	35.63
	c_2		34.54	33.84
South Africa	c_1		23.25	24.04
	c_2		8.72	8.21
	c_3		22.37	23.11
	c_4		8.59	8.10
Sudan	c_1		57.97	58.76
	c_2		48.09	48.07
	c_3		48.94	58.72
	c_4		41.71	48.04
United Arab Republic	c_1		66.88	67.70
	c_2		46.08	48.27

Caribbean and Central America

		1962	1963	1964
Costa Rica	c_1		44.71	42.89
	c_2		35.26	33.55
	c_3		41.73	40.11
	c_4		33.38	31.82
Dominican Republic	c_1		56.84	58.55
	c_2		43.48	43.87
	c_3		54.90	56.40
	c_4		42.33	42.65
El Salvador	c_1		50.09	50.62
	c_2		29.88	28.18
	c_3		47.84	48.59
	c_4		29.06	27.54
Guatamala	c_1		56.24	56.59
	c_2		37.87	35.19
Honduras	c_1		53.60	51.45
	c_2		37.43	35.95
Mexico	c_1		42.49	41.97
	c_2		24.99	23.71

South America

		1962	1963	1964
Argentina	c_1		59.06	57.58
	c_2		41.18	39.69
	c_3		51.84	49.64
	c_4		37.54	35.75
Brazil	c_1		25.57	23.62
	c_2		24.89	23.04
	c_3		24.51	22.27
	c_4		23.88	21.75
Chile	c_1		39.81	39.62
	c_2		26.38	27.63
	c_3		30.43	29.23
	c_4		21.90	22.15
Colombia	c_1		34.58	34.75
	c_2		25.46	26.58
Ecuador	c_1		47.05	46.85
	c_2		38.67	38.26
	c_3		42.83	44.36
	c_4		35.77	36.59
Peru	c_1		54.22	57.71
	c_2		30.63	31.96

Southeast Asia

		1962	1963	1964
Burma	c_1		81.79	83.47
	c_2		77.08	80.03
Ceylon	c_1		55.57	53.11
	c_2		34.50	32.97
India	c_1		70.46	68.51
	c_2		47.54	46.56
Pakistan	c_1		60.75	57.88
	c_2		44.33	41.27
	c_3		60.51	57.68
	c_4		44.21	41.16
Philippines	c_1		58.83	58.52
	c_2		30.84	28.69
	c_3		53.39	53.15
	c_4		27.86	26.10
Thailand	c_1		56.40	56.42
	c_2		37.72	36.32

Supplement to Table B-1

		1962	1963	1964
Europe				
Greece	c_1		78.74	79.58
	c_2		36.99	38.95
	c_3		72.10	73.53
	c_4		35.46	37.44
Iceland	c_1		37.03	35.25
	c_2		10.65	10.59
Ireland	c_1		24.57	22.33
	c_2		9.57	8.77
Portugal	c_1		29.82	27.24
	c_2		24.87	22.38
Spain	c_1	35.57	35.59	34.87
	c_2	17.67	17.37	16.68
Turkey	c_1		73.25	72.03
	c_2		36.41	36.40
Middle East				
Iran	c_1		42.97	42.49
	c_2		26.22	24.35
Iraq	c_1	65.52	73.12	74.23
	c_2	49.84	55.99	56.49
Israel	c_1		32.65	34.58
	c_2		28.89	30.44
Jordan	c_1		62.76	59.96
	c_2		48.12	44.52
	c_3		55.35	53.52
	c_4		43.64	40.87
Lebanon a/	c_1		24.72	
	c_2		21.71	
Syria	c_1		79.98	81.03
	c_2		76.02	77.40
	c_3		75.58	77.05
	c_4		72.03	73.76

a/ In April 1,1964 the Bank of
Lebanon was established,and no
data consistent with 1963 and
earlier years have yet been
published.

Table B-2. Regression Coefficient of the Trend of the Currency Ratio,[a] and the t Value[b]
of the Logarithms of the Regression Coefficient[c]

	B.1	B.2	B.3	B.4	T.1	T.2	T.3	T.4
AFRICA								
Ethiopia	0.9967100	0.9882300	0.	0.	1.5298800	5.5742100	0.	0.
Ghana	0.9711300	0.9655200	0.	0.	5.3979300	8.2441500	0.	0.
Morocco	0.9887700	0.9847400	0.	0.	1.6675900	1.9634600	0.	0.
South Africa	1.0281500	0.9865400	1.0269300	0.9865000	6.8637200	3.2404600	6.6134500	3.2731300
Sudan	0.9599700	0.9536100	0.9568000	0.9513000	14.4788400	14.5424600	8.0277300	9.3383400
United Arab Republic	1.0128500	0.9994100	0.	0.	3.0880900	0.1452000	0.	0.
Arithmetic Average	0.9929300	0.9796750	0.9918650	0.9689000	5.5043420	5.6183230	7.3205900	6.3057350
Geometric Average	0.9926591	0.9795539	0.9912450	0.9687401	4.0209270	2.9180566	7.2863560	5.5286160
CARIBBEAN AND CENTRAL AMERICA								
Costa Rica	0.9849300	0.9732000	0.9846400	0.9734400	5.4689600	9.7756100	5.0046800	8.9123300
Dominican Republic	1.0127500	1.0083200	1.0167700	1.0067700	2.8541600	1.3975900	2.3843900	1.1411800
El Salvador	0.9769600	0.9504500	0.9780600	0.9525300	6.3157900	23.0577100	6.0410700	22.1997700
Guatemala	0.9863600	0.9693100	0.	0.	3.9240300	7.4952900	0.	0.
Honduras	1.0075300	0.9930100	0.	0.	2.2036300	1.4389600	0.	0.
Mexico	0.9899100	0.9707500	0.	0.	5.2605200	11.5891300	0.	0.
Arithmetic Average	0.9930733	0.9775066	0.9911233	0.9775800	4.3378480	9.1257150	4.4767130	10.7510900
Geometric Average	0.9929916	0.9773323	0.9910239	0.9773258	4.0608630	5.8327210	4.1618760	6.0892610
EUROPE								
Greece	1.0073300	0.9274200	1.0056500	0.9302200	2.6911200	10.9995600	2.0984700	10.5435900
Iceland	0.9547400	0.9456100	0.	0.	7.2860600	11.9159300	0.	0.
Ireland	0.9832200	0.9854500	0.	0.	3.5645800	2.8019800	0.	0.
Portugal	0.9932200	0.9847100	0.	0.	2.2630100	6.5751200	0.	0.
Spain	0.9823000	0.9637500	0.	0.	5.4723100	8.0932900	0.	0.
Turkey	0.9920900	0.9758500	0.	0.	2.5180400	5.5922700	0.	0.
Arithmetic Average	0.9854833	0.9637983	1.0056500	0.9302200	3.9658530	7.6630250	2.0984700	10.5435900
Geometric Average	0.9853519	0.9635623	1.0056500	0.9302200	3.6007440	6.9145530	2.0984700	10.5435900
MIDDLE EAST								
Iran	0.9588000	0.9398200	0.	0.	4.5442700	12.3280900	0.	0.
Iran	0.9941000	0.9862700	0.	0.	1.6410000	4.0355100	0.	0.

	1	2	3	4	5	6	7	8
Syria	0.9949700	0.9904200	0.9829200	0.9791200		1.3474000	2.4358700	5.1662200
Arithmetic Average	0.9866516	0.9763183	0.9893650	0.9804100	2.1474320	4.6451670	2.5652450	4.2668300
Geometric Average	0.9865105	0.9761148	0.9893440	0.9804092	1.5958860	2.8953300	1.8656020	4.1709630
SOUTH AMERICA								
Argentina	1.0113500	1.0167100	1.0085500	1.0140000	3.7998800	3.9160700	2.3453600	3.0973000
Brazil	0.9772000	0.9897600	0.9734400	0.9853000	7.2031300	3.0688200	8.2770000	4.3302600
Chile	1.0103700	0.9965000	0.9985900	0.9887400	2.1801600	0.4884100	0.3779000	1.8079400
Colombia	0.9789900	0.9753100	0.	0.	7.6178700	5.8134800	0.	0.
Ecuador	0.9927100	0.9867700	0.9913600	0.9859200	6.7368500	15.5310000	7.8881600	16.3072100
Peru	1.0061700	0.9929200	0.	0.	2.5429800	2.3276600	0.	0.
Arithmetic Average	0.9961336	0.9929950	0.9929850	0.9934900	5.0134780	5.1908970	4.7221050	6.3856770
Geometric Average	0.9960311	0.9929168	0.9929018	0.9934192	4.4521390	3.2748520	2.7580920	4.4592840
SOUTHEAST ASIA								
Burma	1.0026300	0.9980700	0.	0.	1.3180800	0.9886000	0.	0.
Ceylon	1.0269700	1.0123500	0.	0.	4.6057600	2.5754000	0.	0.
India	1.0041300	0.9821200	0.	0.	8.2699400	10.9016200	0.	0.
Pakistan	0.9997200	0.9916300	1.0006100	0.9924800	0.1816200	3.0193500	0.2902100	2.3120200
Philippines	0.9918000	0.9652500	0.9963100	0.9706500	4.2779700	11.6415900	1.5645300	8.0675200
Thailand	0.9782000	0.9568600	0.	0.	7.6386500	9.2845600	0.	0.
Arithmetic Average	1.0005750	0.9843800	0.9984600	0.9815650	4.3820030	6.4018530	0.9273700	5.1897700
Geometric Average	1.0004680	0.9841977	0.9984577	0.9815043	2.5844050	4.5656980	0.6738266	4.3188270
Arithmetic Average	0.9924741000	0.9791121000	0.9935997000	0.9784764000	4.2251590000	6.4408290000	4.0003030000	7.1331600000
Geometric Average	0.9932316000	0.9789062000	0.9934494000	0.9782419000	3.2029090000	4.1481480000	2.6242010000	5.1541340000
Variance	0.0003020249	0.0004003566	0.0002899117	0.0004548657	8.0501620000	26.1316900000	8.1237880000	34.0212300000
Standard Deviation	0.0173788600	0.0200089100	0.0170267900	0.0213275800	2.8372810000	5.1119170000	2.8502260000	5.8327720000
Third Moment	-0.0000009232	-0.0000041426	-0.0000011492	-0.0000055667	28.4819700000	143.4663000000	4.8163130000	254.6163000000
Fourth Moment	0.0000002481	0.0000004717	0.0000002478	0.0000006227	356.3327000000	2784.4880000000	101.3497000000	44441.5710000000
Relative Skewness	0.0309364200	0.2674238000	0.0541961900	0.3292658000	1.5449850000	1.1534460000	0.0432667000	1.6465310000
Relative Kurtosis	2.7200290000	2.9427180000	2.9487930000	3.0097560000	5.4985290000	4.0776520000	1.5356960000	3.8373960000

a/ The regression coefficient is the value of B derived from the trend equation $Y = AB^x$.
b/ The t value is equal to the quotient of the log of B by the standard deviation of the log of B.
c/ The index number following the period indicates the currency ratio from which the variable was computed.

Table B-3. Preliminary Variables R_1,[a/] R_2,[b/] R_3,[c/] Used for the Computations of the "Efficiency" of the Series[d/][e/]

	$R_{1.1}$	$R_{1.2}$	$R_{1.3}$	$R_{1.4}$	$R_{2.1}$	$R_{2.2}$	$R_{2.3}$	$R_{2.4}$	$R_{3.1}$	$R_{3.2}$	$R_{3.3}$	$R_{3.4}$
AFRICA												
Ethiopia	3.54	3.34	0.	0.	-0.02	-0.81	0.	0.	-0.14	-0.88	0.	0.
Ghana	5.05	4.67	0.	0.	-2.39	-2.74	0.	0.	-2.65	-3.00	0.	0.
Morocco	1.98	3.03	0.	0.	-0.74	-0.91	0.	0.	-1.35	-1.90	0.	0.
South Africa	5.89	3.57	5.83	3.54	2.73	-0.99	2.55	-1.01	3.23	-1.08	3.09	-1.08
Sudan	3.00	3.63	5.98	6.04	-2.84	-3.29	-3.47	-3.79	-3.20	-3.64	-3.43	-3.80
United Arab Republic	6.03	6.24	0.	0.	2.55	0.48	0.	0.	1.40	-0.05	0.	0.
Arithmetic Mean	4.25	4.08	5.90	4.79	-0.12	-1.38	-0.46	-2.40	-0.45	-1.76	-0.17	-2.44
Geometric Mean	3.95	3.95	5.90	4.63	0.95	1.21	2.97	1.96	1.39	1.01	3.26	2.02
CARIBBEAN AND CENTRAL AMERICA												
Costa Rica	3.14	3.52	3.08	3.44	-1.94	-2.70	-2.06	-2.76	-1.43	-2.33	-1.45	-2.31
Dominican Republic	7.87	6.31	7.58	6.25	2.11	2.05	1.91	1.88	1.40	1.16	1.21	1.00
El Salvador	2.89	3.81	3.01	3.77	-1.80	-3.81	-1.83	-3.77	-1.79	-3.73	-1.75	-3.64
Guatemala	3.53	4.41	0.	0.	-0.84	-2.32	0.	0.	-0.92	-2.33	0.	0.
Honduras	3.95	4.83	0.	0.	1.09	-0.40	0.	0.	0.75	-0.66	0.	0.
Mexico	3.73	3.87	0.	0.	-1.04	-2.52	0.	0.	-0.95	-2.59	0.	0.
Arithmetic Mean	4.18	4.46	4.55	4.49	-0.40	-1.62	-0.66	-1.55	-0.49	-1.74	-0.67	-1.65
Geometric Mean	3.93	4.37	4.12	4.33	1.38	1.92	1.93	2.69	1.15	1.85	1.45	2.03
EUROPE												
Greece	2.18	5.05	1.95	4.81	0.58	-5.05	0.57	-4.81	0.90	-5.77	0.73	-5.59
Iceland	6.95	5.24	0.	0.	-2.83	-3.96	0.	0.	-3.72	-4.58	0.	0.
Ireland	6.44	6.99	0.	0.	-1.68	-1.46	0.	0.	-1.54	-1.30	0.	0.
Portugal	3.09	3.35	0.	0.	-0.27	-1.11	0.	0.	-0.57	-1.36	0.	0.
Spain	2.83	4.19	0.	0.	-1.73	-3.45	0.	0.	-1.71	-3.31	0.	0.
Turkey	2.37	3.25	0.	0.	-0.82	-2.28	0.	0.	-0.93	-2.29	0.	0.
Arithmetic Mean	3.98	4.68	1.95	4.81	-1.12	-2.89	0.57	-4.81	-1.26	-3.10	0.73	-5.59
Geometric Mean	3.56	4.51	1.95	4.81	1.00	2.52	0.57	4.81	1.29	2.66	0.73	5.59
MIDDLE EAST												
Iran	5.28	5.44	0.	0.	-2.50	-4.28	0.	0.	-3.49	-4.85	0.	0.
Iraq	2.20	3.24	0.	0.	-0.59	-1.57	0.	0.	-0.49	-1.17	0.	0.
Israel	9.66	9.02	0.	0.	1.32	0.83	0.	0.	0.88	0.23	0.	0.
Jordan	4.36	4.88	4.62	4.69	0.10	-1.49	-0.26	-1.66	-0.32	-1.68	-0.42	-1.67

Syria	4.17	4.65	4.07	4.45	0.33	-0.10	[illegible]	[illegible]	[illegible]	[illegible]	[illegible]	[illegible]
Arithmetic Mean	5.50	5.72	4.34	4.57	-0.71	-1.68	-0.47	-1.34	-1.11	-1.97	-1.03	-1.83
Geometric Mean	4.96	5.43	4.33	4.57	0.75	1.19	0.42	1.30	0.95	1.40	0.83	1.82
SOUTH AMERICA												
Argentina	3.63	5.58	4.39	5.72	1.85	2.59	2.28	2.83	1.36	2.16	1.17	1.90
Brazil	3.49	3.67	3.57	3.55	-2.31	-1.46	-2.57	-1.80	-2.06	-1.05	-2.40	-1.48
Chile	4.49	6.31	5.67	6.20	1.44	-0.67	-0.33	-1.57	1.44	-0.23	-0.28	-1.23
Colombia	4.22	5.64	0.	0.	-2.01	-2.17	0.	0.	-2.02	-2.38	0.	0.
Ecuador	1.73	1.95	1.92	1.78	-0.78	-1.21	-0.77	-1.19	-0.69	-1.16	-0.83	-1.25
Peru	4.04	4.04	0.	0.	1.06	-0.70	0.	0.	0.26	-1.00	0.	0.
Arithmetic Mean	3.60	4.53	3.89	4.31	-0.12	-0.60	-0.35	-0.43	-0.29	-0.61	-0.58	-0.51
Geometric Mean	3.45	4.23	3.61	3.87	1.48	1.29	1.10	1.76	1.06	1.06	0.90	1.44
SOUTHEAST ASIA												
Burma	3.39	2.82	0.	0.	0.37	-0.06	0.	0.	0.37	-0.07	0.	0.
Ceylon	6.46	4.62	0.	0.	2.48	1.28	0.	0.	3.20	1.39	0.	0.
India	1.03	1.73	0.	0.	0.39	-1.35	0.	0.	0.47	-1.47	0.	0.
Pakistan	1.97	2.79	2.67	3.42	-0.17	-1.07	-0.20	-1.07	-0.08	-0.83	0.03	-0.74
Philippines	3.46	3.63	4.20	4.10	-0.94	-2.93	0.18	-2.22	-0.57	-2.73	-0.21	-2.38
Thailand	2.79	4.17	0.	0.	-1.82	-3.75	0.	0.	-1.99	-3.64	0.	0.
Arithmetic Mean	3.18	3.30	3.44	3.76	0.05	-1.31	-0.01	-1.65	0.23	-1.23	-0.09	-1.56
Geometric Mean	2.74	3.14	3.35	3.75	0.69	1.04	0.19	1.55	0.61	1.02	0.08	1.33
Arithmetic Mean	4.12	4.46	4.18	4.41	-0.40	-1.58	-0.34	-1.57	-0.56	-1.73	-0.44	-1.73
Geometric Mean	3.71	4.22	3.87	4.21	1.00	1.45	0.93	1.98	1.04	1.40	0.82	1.83
Variance	3.58	2.24	2.52	1.57	2.66	3.04	2.97	3.89	2.76	2.94	2.61	3.30
Standard Deviation	1.89	1.50	1.59	1.25	1.63	1.74	1.72	1.97	1.66	1.71	1.62	1.82
Third Moment	6.29	2.60	1.68	-0.22	1.16	1.53	0.24	4.94	1.12	-0.40	1.09	-0.25
Fourth Moment	44.83	18.95	15.43	5.91	14.54	25.68	19.79	48.44	21.10	25.53	19.47	34.60
Relative Skewness	0.86	0.61	0.18	0.01	0.07	0.08	0.00	0.41	0.06	0.01	0.07	0.00
Relative Kurtosis	3.50	3.79	2.42	2.39	2.05	2.77	2.24	3.20	2.78	2.96	2.86	3.17

a/ R_1 represents in percentages the total length of the path travelled per year by the currency ratio from the beginning till the end of the period.

b/ R_2 represents the arithmetic average, expressed in percentages, of the annual rate of change when the currency ratio for the first and the last years of the period are compared.

c/ R_3 represents the arithmetic average, expressed in percentages, of the annual rate of change when the average currency ratio for the first three years is compared with the average currency ratio for the last three years.

d/ The index number following the period indicates the currency ratio from which the variable was computed. Countries for which no c_3 and c_4 ratios were computed appear with zero under the columns where the second subscript is 3 or 4.

e/ Geometric averages in this table are computed from the absolute value of the variables.

Table B-4. R_4,[a] R_5,[b] - Indices of the "Efficiency" of the Series[c] [d]

	$R_{4.1}$	$R_{4.2}$	$R_{4.3}$	$R_{4.4}$	$R_{5.1}$	$R_{5.2}$	$R_{5.3}$	$R_{5.4}$
AFRICA								
Ethiopia	-0.60	-24.29	0.	0.	-3.87	-26.45	0.	0.
Ghana	-47.34	-58.57	0.	0.	-52.52	-64.22	0.	0.
Morocco	-37.58	-30.16	0.	0.	-68.01	-62.69	0.	0.
South Africa	46.45	-27.70	43.74	-28.51	54.87	-30.29	53.08	-30.42
Sudan	-94.79	-90.54	-58.04	-62.83	-106.95	-100.08	-57.37	-62.88
United Arab Republic	42.22	7.69	0.	0.	23.19	-0.85	0.	0.
Arithmetic Mean	-15.27	-37.26	-7.15	-45.67	-25.55	-47.43	-2.14	-46.65
Geometric Mean	24.12	30.64	50.38	42.33	35.13	25.47	55.18	43.73
CARIBBEAN AND CENTRAL AMERICA								
Costa Rica	-61.67	-76.67	-66.95	-80.12	-45.56	-66.14	-47.11	-66.99
Dominican Republic	26.80	32.44	25.17	30.12	17.84	18.38	15.91	16.07
El Salvador	-62.32	-100.00	-60.78	-100.00	-62.05	-97.84	-58.21	-96.48
Guatemala	-23.69	-52.67	0.	0.	-25.96	-52.92	0.	0.
Honduras	27.50	-8.36	0.	0.	18.93	-13.57	0.	0.
Mexico	-27.89	-65.23	0.	0.	-25.48	-66.90	0.	0.
Arithmetic Mean	-20.21	-45.08	-34.19	-50.00	-20.38	-46.50	-29.81	-49.13
Geometric Mean	35.10	43.88	46.79	62.26	29.29	42.29	35.20	47.00
EUROPE								
Greece	26.45	-100.00	29.25	-100.00	41.21	-114.43	37.74	-116.17
Iceland	-40.72	-75.62	0.	0.	-53.51	-87.29	0.	0.
Ireland	-26.09	-20.94	0.	0.	-23.91	-18.56	0.	0.
Portugal	-8.60	-33.03	0.	0.	-18.46	-40.58	0.	0.
Spain	-61.14	-82.28	0.	0.	-60.46	-78.99	0.	0.
Turkey	-34.40	-70.14	0.	0.	-39.20	-70.40	0.	0.
Arithmetic Mean	-24.08	-63.67	29.25	-100.00	-25.72	-68.38	37.74	-116.17
Geometric Mean	28.25	55.80	29.25	100.00	36.35	58.92	37.74	116.17
MIDDLE EAST								
Iran	-47.44	-78.64	0.	0.	-66.13	-89.17	0.	0.
Iraq	-26.59	-48.32	0.	0.	-22.18	-36.08	0.	0.
Israel	13.70	9.17	0.	0.	9.14	2.52	0.	0.

SOUTH AMERICA							
Argentina	51.00	46.38	51.89	49.51	37.56	38.73	26.57	33.25
Brazil	-66.27	-39.87	-71.93	-50.69	-59.12	-28.65	-67.06	-41.75
Chile	32.17	-10.54	-5.73	-25.40	31.98	-3.60	-4.91	-19.79
Colombia	-47.59	-38.37	0.	0.	-47.91	-42.14	0.	0.
Ecuador	-45.04	-62.12	-40.46	-66.60	-39.57	-59.51	-43.32	-70.38
Peru	26.33	-17.37	0.	0.	6.45	-24.76	0.	0.
Arithmetic Mean	-8.24	-20.32	-16.56	-23.29	-11.77	-19.99	-22.18	-24.67
Geometric Mean	42.79	30.51	30.50	45.39	30.89	25.07	24.81	37.29
SOUTHEAST ASIA							
Burma	10.96	-2.21	0.	0.	10.88	-2.41	0.	0.
Ceylon	38.38	27.67	0.	0.	49.48	29.99	0.	0.
India	38.24	-77.62	0.	0.	46.03	-84.73	0.	0.
Pakistan	-8.81	-38.36	-7.59	-31.40	-4.16	-29.87	1.12	-21.57
Philippines	-27.18	-80.55	4.24	-54.20	-16.51	-75.00	-4.99	-58.07
Thailand	-65.23	-89.98	0.	0.	-71.16	-87.23	0.	0.
Arithmetic Mean	-2.27	-43.51	-1.67	-42.80	2.43	-41.54	-1.94	-39.82
Geometric Mean	25.12	33.12	5.68	41.25	22.24	32.59	2.36	35.39
Arithmetic Mean	-14.17	-40.51	-12.83	-41.32	-17.30	-43.59	-14.15	-43.97
Geometric Mean	27.03	34.44	23.93	46.95	28.11	33.18	21.29	43.58
Variance	1494.66	1447.42	1611.80	1713.70	1572.06	1403.55	1388.09	1476.15
Standard Deviation	38.66	38.04	40.15	41.40	39.65	37.46	37.26	38.42
Third Moment	1979.57	20443.53	-107.78	45405.46	2545.26	11431.26	10744.12	10272.27
Fourth Moment	4218212.75	4911666.50	4565306.81	8639068.37	5513229.62	4652803.37	3484508.03	6063005.50
Relative Skewness	0.00	0.14	0.00	0.41	0.00	0.05	0.04	0.03
Relative Kurtosis	1.89	2.34	1.76	2.94	2.23	2.36	1.81	2.78

a/ $R_4 = \dfrac{R_2}{R_1}$ x 100. For the meaning of R_2 and R_1, see Table B-3.

b/ $R_5 = \dfrac{R_3}{R_1}$ x 100. For the meaning of R_3, see Table B-3.

c/ The index following the period indicates the currency ratio from which the variable was computed. Countries for which no c_3 and c_4 ratios were computed appear with zero under the columns where the second subscript is 3 or 4.

d/ Geometric averages in this table are computed from the absolute value of the variables.

Table B-5

Coefficients of Linear Correlation[a] Computed From c_1,[b] and PCI Index,[c] and the Percentage Annual Rate of Change[d] of PCI, 1948-61.

Country	Period	Correlation Coefficient	Annual Rate of Change of PCI
AFRICA			
U.A.R.	1952-58	0.525 ns	1.915
CENTRAL AMERICA			
Guatemala	1950-61	-0.815 s	2.051
Honduras	1948-60	.783 s	1.540
Mexico	1950-60	- .564 ns	1.859
EUROPE			
Greece	1953-61	.612 ns	5.292
Iceland	1951-60	- .742 s	3.481
Ireland	1948-61	- .591 s	1.858
Portugal	1950-61	- .281 ns	3.664
Spain	1950-59	- .875 s	4.157
Turkey	1949-61	- .705 s	3.255
MIDDLE EAST			
Israel	1950-59	- .130 ns	6.109
Syria	1953-61	.810 s	-2.188
SOUTH AMERICA			
Argentina	1950-61	- .275 ns	.007
Brazil	1948-61	- .904 s	2.683
Chile	1950-61	.278 ns	1.285
Colombia	1950-60	- .873 s	2.584
Ecuador	1950-61	- .782 s	1.450
Peru	1950-58	.233 ns	.795
SOUTHEAST ASIA			
Burma	1950-61	.346 ns	3.937
Ceylon	1950-60	.592 ns	.484
India	1950-60	.869 s	1.356
Pakistan	1949-61	.224 ns	.585
Philippines	1950-61	- .511 ns	2.634
Thailand	1952-61	- .459 ns	1.327

a. The letters ns and s written at the corner of each box denote whether the correlation coefficient for the given row and column was found not significant (ns) or significant (s) at 5 per cent level of significance. The reader is cautioned not to put too much emphasis on the results of the test, since the observations are time series.

b. $c_1 = \dfrac{\text{currency in circulation outside the banks}}{\text{currency in circulation outside the banks + demand deposits of the private sector}}$

c. PCI is Per Capita Income

d. Annual rate of change is equal to 100 (B-1), where B is derived from the trend equation $Y = AB^X$.

Table B-6. Correlation Coefficients[a] Computed From c_1,[b] c_2,[c] and COL,[d] 1948-1962

Area	Year[e]	$c_{1t}=a+b(COL)_t$	$\log c_{1t}=a+b\log(COL)_t$	Detrended $c_{1t}=a+b(CUL)_t$	$c_{2t}=a+b(COL)_t$	$\log c_{2t}=a+b\log(COL)_t$	Detrended $c_{2t}=a+b(CUL)_t$	$c_{1t}=a+b(COL)_{t-1}$	$\log c_{1t}=a+b\log(COL)_{t-1}$	Detrended $c_{1t}=a+b(COL)_{t-1}$	$c_{2t}=a+b(COL)_{t-1}$	$\log c_{2t}=a+b\log(COL)_{t-1}$	Detrended $c_{2t}=a+b(COL)_{t-1}$
AFRICA [f]													
Ethiopia	1950-62	-.825 s	-.798 s	-.110 ns	-.858 s	-.848 s	.005 ns	-.799 s	-.752 s	-.043 ns	-.868 s	-.833 s	-.073 ns
Ghana	1958-62	-.729 ns	-.729 ns	-.343 ns	-.818 ns	-.822 ns	-.587 ns	-.937 s	-.939 s	-.280 ns	-.876 ns	-.881 ns	.300 ns
Morocco	1948-62	.941 s	.954 s	.785 s	-.514 ns	-.476 ns	.925 s	-.912 s	-.930 s	.656 s	-.678 s	-.642 s	.711 s
South Africa	1951-62	-.876 s	-.873 s	.468 ns	-.883 s	-.876 s	.405 ns	-.834 s	-.832 s	.546 ns	-.832 s	-.830 s	.606 ns
Sudan	1950-62	-.209 ns	.232 ns	.381 ns	.475 ns	.460 ns	.473 ns	.210 ns	.218 ns	.286 ns	.107 ns	.103 ns	.101 ns
United Arab Rep.													
CARIBBEAN AND CENTRAL AMERICA													
Costa Rica	1948-62	-.923 s	-.947 s	.832 s	-.971 s	-.973 s	.808 s	-.908 s	-.899 s	-.292 ns	-.935 s	-.912 s	-.232 ns
Dominican Republic	1950-62	.397 ns	.397 ns	.281 ns	.080 ns	.063 ns	-.036 ns	-.121 ns	-.102 ns	-.188 ns	.344 ns	-.338 ns	-.399 ns
El Salvador	1948-62	-.940 s	-.907 s	-.682 s	-.826 s	-.751 s	.286 ns	-.928 s	-.901 s	.584 s	-.840 s	-.769 s	.429 ns
Guatemala	1948-62	-.630 s	-.616 s	-.038 ns	-.670 s	-.650 s	.297 ns	-.678 s	-.667 s	-.132 ns	-.685 s	-.668 s	.275 ns
Honduras	1948-62	.721 s	.749 s	.682 s	-.009 ns	.014 ns	.751 s	.594 ns	.617 s	.604 s	-.323 ns	.307 ns	.594 s
Mexico	1948-62	-.801 s	-.780 s	.199 ns	-.936 s	-.908 s	.445 ns	-.809 s	-.791 s	-.197 ns	-.949 s	-.928 s	.043 ns
EUROPE													
Greece	1953-62	.550 ns	.519 ns	-.337 ns	-.926 s	-.890 s	-.352 ns	.818 s	.814 s	.480 ns	-.927 s	-.903 s	-.308 ns
Iceland	1951-62	-.886 s	-.910 s	-.090 ns	-.944 s	-.938 s	.201 ns	-.881 s	-.906 s	.462 ns	-.945 s	-.939 s	.415 ns
Ireland	1948-62	-.615 s	-.592 s	.475 ns	-.508 ns	-.489 ns	.505 ns	-.685 s	-.660 s	.218 ns	-.611 ns	-.590 s	.201 ns
Portugal	1948-62	-.233 ns	-.252 ns	.758 s	-.636 s	-.699 s	.653 s	-.194 ns	-.213 ns	.554 s	-.681 s	-.693 s	.455 ns
Spain	1950-61	-.694 s	-.727 s	.766 s	-.761 s	-.797 s	.893 s	-.605 s	-.640 s	.723 s	-.762 s	-.800 s	.497 ns
Turkey	1949-62	-.288 ns	-.321 ns	.805 s	-.587 s	-.645 s	.830 s	-.130 ns	-.147 ns	.683 s	-.529 ns	-.580 s	.626 s

	Period												
MIDDLE EAST													
Iran	1952-62	.844 s	-.841 s	.033 ns	-.956 s	-.954 s	.122 ns	-.763 s	-.775 s	.370 ns	-.933 s	-.943 s	.412 ns
Iraq	1950-61	-.134 ns	-.137 ns	.139 ns	-.519 ns	-.525 ns	-.211 ns	.028 ns	.037 ns	.130 ns	-.267 ns	-.267 ns	.035 ns
Israel [f/]	1948-62	.242 ns	.380 ns	.271 ns	.011 ns	.146 ns	.232 ns	-.065 ns	.049 ns	.028 ns	-.332 ns	-.238 ns	-.089 ns
Jordan [f/]													
Lebanon	1950-62	-.879 s	-.861 s	-.639 ns	-.381 s	-.858 s	-.571 s	-.866 s	-.856 s	-.635 ns	-.872 s	-.858 s	-.608 s
Syria	1951-62	-.245 ns	-.247 ns	-.060 ns	-.313 ns	-.316 ns	-.014 ns	-.356 ns	-.350 ns	-.027 ns	-.334 ns	-.328 ns	.072 ns
SOUTH AMERICA													
Argentina	1948-62	.394 ns	.659 s	.221 ns	.460 ns	.712 s	.254 ns	.337 ns	.597 s	-.050 ns	.389 ns	.643 s	-.084 ns
Brazil	1948-62	-.899 s	-.932 s	-.085 ns	-.811 s	-.729 s	-.118 ns	-.919 s	-.919 s	.012 ns	-.792 s	-.698 s	-.029 ns
Chile	1948-62	.230 ns	.486 ns	.220 ns	-.410 ns	-.090 ns	.211 ns	.066 ns	.305 ns	-.020 ns	-.546 ns	-.266 ns	-.067 ns
Colombia	1948-62	-.845 s	-.875 s	.379 ns	-.762 s	-.811 s	.542 s	-.839 s	-.877 s	.272 ns	-.755 s	-.816 s	.375 s
Ecuador	1948-62	-.718 s	-.703 s	.244 ns	-.806 s	-.794 s	.439 ns	-.720 s	-.709 s	.053 ns	-.829 s	-.815 s	-.051 ns
Peru	1948-62	.565 s	.555 s	.043 ns	-.490 ns	-.551 s	.475 ns	.448 ns	.411 ns	-.128 ns	-.483 ns	-.549 s	.136 ns
SOUTHEAST ASIA													
Burma	1948-62	-.006 ns	-.021 ns	.030 ns	.190 ns	.175 ns	.175 ns	.017 ns	.045 ns	.075 ns	.077 ns	.101 ns	.054 ns
Ceylon	1948-62	.698 s	.680 s	-.134 ns	.537 s	.506 ns	-.041 ns	.693 s	.682 s	-.187 ns	.475 ns	.446 ns	-.281 ns
India	1948-62	.868 s	.862 s	.307 ns	-.891 s	-.897 s	-.343 ns	.857 s	.852 s	.365 ns	-.838 s	-.844 s	-.164 ns
Pakistan	1948-62	-.153 ns	-.139 ns	-.367 ns	-.682 s	-.661 s	.313 ns	-.389 ns	-.366 ns	.444 ns	.817 s	-.791 s	-.550 s
Philippines	1948-62	-.425 ns	-.431 ns	-.079 ns	-.554 s	-.597 s	-.383 ns	-.172 ns	-.175 ns	.064 ns	-.346 ns	-.391 ns	-.138 ns
Thailand	1952-62	-.856 s	-.839 s	.307 ns	-.891 s	-.858 s	.350 ns	-.823 s	-.807 s	.358 ns	-.874 s	-.844 s	-.339 ns

a/ The letters s and ns inserted in each box indicate the result of the t test with 95 per cent confidence interval. Thus, s indicates the coefficient in the given box was found significant; ns indicates the coefficient was found not significant. The reader is cautioned not to put too much emphasis on the results of the test, since the observations are time series.

b/ $c_1 = \dfrac{\text{currency in circulation outside the banks}}{\text{currency in circulation outside the banks} + \text{demand deposits held by the private sector}}$

c/ $c_2 = \dfrac{\text{currency in circulation outside the banks}}{\text{currency in circulation outside the banks} + \text{demand deposits held by the private sector} + \text{savings and time deposits of the private sector}}$

d/ COL = Cost of living index, with 1953 taken as base year.

e/ For correlation with the cost of living lagged, the beginning year is one year later.

f/ No correlations were computed since the cost of living indexes for these countries were not available.

Table B-7. Savings and Time Deposits as Percentage of Money Supply a/

Country	1948	1949	1950	1951	1952	1953	1954	1955	1956	1957	1958	1959	1960	1961	1962	Annual Rate of Growth b/
AFRICA																
Ethicpia	2.10	4.35	3.68	3.92	7.02	6.24	9.18	9.36	13.05	12.91	11.41	11.74	12.79	13.81		13.98
Ghana			18.25	18.81	18.64	20.22	19.71	20.11	21.07	25.26	28.46	28.42	26.83	20.04	25.49	3.22
Morocco											6.93	5.04	8.59	7.89	7.68	6.76
South Africa	64.31	72.34	71.14	73.14	81.19	83.91	95.31	113.50	125.86	138.61	146.78	156.14	170.84	174.99	163.66	8.29
Sudan			6.92	10.79	9.38	8.04	13.85	9.96	9.41	11.46	12.48	16.13	16.47	16.20	16.46	6.53
United Arab Republic			15.38	15.25	17.50	20.39	22.37	22.72	19.49	20.63	26.88	29.68	28.34	28.24	42.46	7.11
CARIBBEAN AND CENTRAL AMERICA																
Costa Rica	9.01	10.47	11.88	12.42	13.01	13.84	14.22	17.61	19.17	20.14	23.13	25.04	25.80	26.94	27.64	8.55
Dominican Republic			22.30	20.59	21.25	22.33	39.97	46.14	50.13	53.19	37.91	43.72	27.15	22.28	23.05	2.01
El Salvador	1.06	2.01	1.52	1.43	1.02	1.55	1.77	2.53	4.02	7.61	11.85	19.30	27.77	46.22	61.89	34.79
Guatemala	10.07	12.90	14.41	14.85	12.38	14.19	10.75	12.50	17.47	20.23	26.17	27.97	34.47	39.01	44.06	10.24
Honduras	14.98	15.86	15.52	14.08	14.00	14.88	15.06	19.03	23.42	25.51	24.82	27.81	33.53	36.16	40.41	8.06
Mexico	25.57	25.25	24.43	28.68	28.72	32.14	43.66	40.86	40.62	40.36	39.93	47.35	55.84	60.98	65.84	7.18
EUROPE																
Greece						3.67	6.35	8.91	24.97	49.89	66.54	80.90	82.80	86.39	99.79	46.45
Iceland	181.07	181.55	179.59	152.54	164.15	181.78	213.15	155.41	161.59	158.16	154.27	161.30	200.18	196.31	208.52	1.51
Ireland				173.71	169.94	172.38	171.96	171.11	172.46	166.77	173.65	173.99	170.82	171.95	170.38	-.35
Portugal	3.67	3.45	3.57	3.50	4.07	4.73	5.25	6.29	6.90	7.56	8.72	9.97	12.75	14.87	18.13	12.90
Spain			52.64	54.63	61.57	67.75	72.30	75.30	73.39	70.13	69.64	72.34	94.63	99.07		4.67

MIDDLE EAST

	1	2	3	4	5	6	7	8	9	10	11	12	13	14	Rate b/
Iran	8.26	17.12	23.13	17.30	17.94	19.88	20.38	22.51	20.87	20.09	24.52	25.27	39.35	53.72	9.30
Iraq	8.71	11.51	10.72	22.58	20.93	19.22	21.18	22.80	27.04	23.35	24.80	30.30	32.40	15.01	4.19
Israel	1.50	5.24	9.56	14.86	15.58	18.01	16.97	16.84	19.61	19.14	20.44	20.14	18.75	27.17	6.21
Jordan				6.66	7.55	8.18	10.28	12.84	15.21	15.24	17.69	17.61	21.33	13.18	14.90
Lebanon			1.48	2.83	4.59	5.65	7.03	6.70	6.33	6.53	7.82	10.13	11.51	6.40	18.39
Syria					2.33	3.12	3.64	4.95	4.79	4.52	5.14	5.93	8.15	6.37	12.75

SOUTH AMERICA

	1	2	3	4	5	6	7	8	9	10	11	12	13	14	15	Rate b/
Argentina	51.78	50.28	44.26	39.42	38.20	37.20	37.94	36.88	46.00	42.38	40.78	31.99	34.28	37.33	40.31	-1.77
Brazil	20.89	20.83	19.55	18.67	16.08	14.34	13.45	10.92	9.56	8.36	7.18	5.46	4.70	3.54	2.82	-13.48
Chile	20.00	23.75	30.49	30.89	27.45	27.54	24.34	18.74	18.50	25.24	25.99	45.23	44.32	48.55	59.09	5.37
Colombia	24.70	19.33	22.82	27.15	30.20	27.68	35.16	33.33	36.83	29.07	26.82	30.50	30.66	29.02	28.63	1.87
Ecuador	14.15	14.64	14.81	15.49	14.89	16.70	17.61	19.98	20.48	22.61	21.79	22.07	21.24	22.60	22.40	3.98
Peru	32.46	36.81	39.00	41.58	48.06	47.19	48.87	56.25	56.02	62.73	60.64	50.23	55.78	54.19	68.74	4.20

SOUTHEAST ASIA

	1	2	3	4	5	6	7	8	9	10	11	12	13	14	15	Rate b/
Burma	5.41	5.34	6.88	7.43	7.01	6.24	9.03	10.84	7.67	9.04	9.00	14.07	11.25	11.24	11.86	5.99
Ceylon	41.68	37.19	32.29	35.72	44.05	47.19	44.14	42.28	45.71	54.07	57.83	58.85	64.83	61.44	61.89	4.52
India	17.04	18.92	20.34	21.73	25.31	27.02	28.32	29.75	31.78	39.25	48.43	55.38	52.39	52.53	52.14	9.43
Pakistan	17.49	19.11	16.81	15.12	17.36	18.18	21.25	20.35	19.84	20.69	21.45	25.23	25.77	28.82	34.86	4.49
Philippines	38.19	39.28	30.95	35.09	37.38	43.47	48.21	51.52	54.98	60.28	61.27	66.69	76.53	88.42	103.32	7.86
Thailand					8.66	9.39	10.56	11.76	13.20	15.00	17.51	20.26	22.82	26.40	42.29	15.39

a/ Money supply defined as currency outside the banks plus private demand deposits.

b/ Annual rate of growth is equal to 100(B-1), where B is derived from the trend equation $y = AB^x$. The rate can be positive or negative, depending on whether the percentages have an upward or downward trend.

Table B-8. Savings and Time Deposits as Percentages of Demand Deposits

Country	1948	1949	1950	1951	1952	1953	1954	1955	1956	1957	1958	1959	1960	1961	1962	Annual Rate of Growth
AFRICA																
Ethiopia	9.24	21.94	15.84	23.16	34.75	31.79	56.52	50.00	64.79	56.41	45.03	53.01	52.71	60.24		12.60
Ghana			78.41	82.61	69.49	68.70	61.04	61.90	69.94	76.25	77.84	82.23	76.27	38.05	56.27	-2.32
Morocco											10.73	7.88	13.44	11.98	11.70	6.12
South Africa	77.57	89.14	87.54	91.47	103.55	108.16	123.73	150.85	167.83	185.79	199.20	209.35	230.33	236.38	214.31	9.13
Sudan			61.92	75.24	52.68	44.76	68.57	43.89	35.09	32.78	33.63	40.37	38.95	38.73	39.71	-4.94
United Arab Republic			28.85	31.31	36.40	40.26	44.80	43.89	40.77	42.40	57.05	57.44	58.98	67.15	108.77	8.73
CARIBBEAN AND CENTRAL AMERICA																
Costa Rica	24.12	23.13	23.60	25.54	25.80	27.75	29.02	34.28	36.34	39.13	44.28	46.49	48.67	49.59	50.86	6.77
Dominican Republic			39.92	37.84	39.77	45.48	79.04	98.63	108.09	112.80	71.73	98.51	52.51	46.23	51.59	3.30
El Salvador	3.53	6.12	4.20	3.90	2.65	3.69	4.08	5.23	8.28	15.19	23.22	37.79	56.88	101.06	129.99	30.35
Guatemala	29.79	41.48	42.29	44.55	43.17	47.58	36.24	31.23	40.77	46.59	63.87	67.64	86.34	98.53	106.03	7.62
Honduras	27.44	32.20	32.06	30.16	31.18	32.91	34.91	42.50	53.74	62.95	58.72	62.43	74.89	77.75	84.72	8.93
Mexico	52.71	53.91	46.25	57.33	58.23	62.34	90.63	77.89	78.34	77.59	77.53	87.63	102.76	110.63	117.58	6.17
EUROPE																
Greece	272.69	273.13	275.69	300.50	337.86	432.51	465.22	274.19	102.03	196.67	265.37	315.69	325.48	343.48	438.50	49.45
Iceland				262.76	264.44	276.27	248.48	267.92	294.08	265.78	252.62	251.98	316.12	301.86	315.57	-2.10
Ireland									263.90	258.43	253.32	246.68	241.58	239.32	229.30	-1.11
Portugal	5.41	5.16	5.23	5.05	5.86	6.72	7.37	8.87	9.80	10.60	12.13	13.79	17.56	21.83	26.21	12.57
Spain			94.32	95.72	104.36	110.44	117.17	118.19	114.92	111.73	108.55	112.20	150.43	154.27		3.46
Turkey		256.93	288.79	269.18	210.99	248.57	234.12	225.12	249.50	291.67	272.97	274.05	285.16	299.76	323.30	1.54

The following table presents index/trend data by region and country (data columns are unlabeled in the source; the final column is the annual rate of growth, footnote a/).

Region / Country															Rate a/
MIDDLE EAST															
Iran	11.40			37.81	38.00	41.16	39.24	41.07	36.38	31.67	38.15	37.79	66.26	90.54	5.62
Iraq		63.28	78.95	73.13	62.79	57.49	61.14	62.59	70.70	66.47	75.07	95.32	102.00		2.86
Israel	12.59	17.44	17.21	16.24	26.57	26.89	30.58	30.38	32.73	30.92	31.85	30.53	29.07	22.26	6.43
Jordan		2.86	13.71	20.54	23.57	27.43	31.42	49.13	49.17	49.48	55.62	49.94	60.13	72.28	14.25
Lebanon			2.37	5.17	8.68	10.98	13.00	13.68	11.19	12.19	12.60	15.78	17.34	19.09	15.98
Syria			4.95	10.61	13.58	15.38	19.44	22.32	20.00	20.14	21.16	25.10	23.50	23.35	11.10
SOUTH AMERICA															
Argentina	101.42	103.88	92.62	95.56	89.60	97.14	96.21	115.03	111.14	104.54	78.75	83.57	91.56	105.05	-.36
Brazil	33.33	31.87	28.76	24.13	21.54	20.78	16.76	14.59	12.17	10.47	7.62	6.49	4.91	3.77	-14.38
Chile	30.49	35.51	52.21	49.65	49.76	42.48	33.02	33.19	43.90	44.83	78.60	75.73	81.80	100.77	6.02
Colombia	48.96	41.15	50.33	56.14	49.48	60.06	56.52	61.02	51.61	46.37	52.02	51.71	46.53	44.47	.20
Ecuador	31.19	32.26	34.49	31.52	35.38	36.92	42.60	43.29	47.77	45.74	43.82	42.44	45.12	43.61	3.17
Peru	58.26	71.16	75.41	86.61	86.41	91.05	105.07	106.31	120.58	124.54	101.35	108.32	100.60	139.90	4.78
SOUTHEAST ASIA															
Burma	16.46	16.33	21.63	22.95	18.58	27.64	30.95	20.08	27.78	25.76	45.69	35.64	36.27	40.37	6.60
Ceylon	69.13	60.10	57.65	73.95	79.92	69.09	66.22	71.27	93.47	114.90	113.91	128.90	135.24	133.06	6.84
India	54.40	59.35	72.37	84.28	92.67	93.40	100.99	108.74	130.04	167.30	198.72	189.24	193.24	189.34	10.52
Pakistan	49.62	56.04	45.41	52.70	55.00	65.80	64.47	67.06	65.60	67.04	75.81	80.20	83.77	94.45	4.48
Philippines	138.18	135.78	120.38	122.38	151.49	166.30	160.06	162.84	185.15	164.40	186.90	231.06	250.44	277.95	6.01
Thailand	19.59	50.61	89.14	31.43	29.89	35.98	41.46	44.16	46.77	50.17	55.76	57.07	64.04	103.76	10.64

a/ The annual rate of growth is expressed in percentages, and is equal to 100(B-1), where B is derived from the trend equation $Y = AB^X$. The rate may be positive or negative depending on whether the trend is upward or downward.

APPENDIX C

DATA FOR THE 1936-62 PERIOD, AND SOURCE

The computations that appear in this appendix are based on data derived in part from the files of the IMF and in part from various issues of the International Financial Statistics.

For remark on the nature of the series, see the last paragraph in the General Remarks section of Appendix B.

Table C-1. Currency Ratio[a], 1936-1962

		1936	1937	1938	1939	1940	1941	1942	1943	1944	1945	1946	1947	1948
AFRICA														
United Arab Republic	c_1				49.44	49.43	51.30	53.46	49.53	44.21	42.09	43.72	44.39	44.23
CENTRAL AMERICA														
Costa Rica	c_1		41.05	47.36	45.68	45.04	48.50	45.95	48.04	47.72	47.93	47.42	51.37	60.11
El Salvador	c_1	72.31	73.64	73.91	74.57	73.83	73.85	68.63	64.79	67.68	58.75	63.95	64.87	67.27
	c_2	69.44	69.84	69.39	70.33	69.91	69.67	61.40	62.12	66.43	58.18	63.17	63.39	66.59
Guatemala	c_1		80.14	63.38	64.58	61.74	68.57	61.85	56.92	60.73	59.17	60.16	62.60	66.19
Mexico	c_1		63.11	68.57	66.45	60.55	61.08	57.29	56.67	53.47	46.88	49.96	51.02	51.50
SOUTH AMERICA														
Argentina	c_1	46.08	45.06	46.43	44.73	43.32	38.63	38.50	38.37	38.21	38.11	40.16	44.28	48.95
Brazil	c_1	41.46	37.23	30.33	33.61	36.75	36.18	33.33	30.77	33.15	34.46	36.68	35.88	35.40
	c_2	32.08	30.97	25.69	25.81	27.04	26.57	24.90	23.53	24.95	25.54	27.50	27.52	26.86
Colombia	c_1	60.48	57.81	57.04	56.16	50.63	53.98	51.29	46.01	48.16	46.30	46.31	47.74	49.54
Ecuador	c_1	48.82	53.62	55.30	56.52	45.98	50.21	48.99	47.15	49.00	50.79	50.14	54.65	54.53
	c_2	42.47	46.84	46.79	46.43	38.83	43.48	42.04	41.21	43.64	43.85	43.59	47.00	47.78

a/ Using: C for currency in circulation outside the banks, DD for demand deposits held by the private sector, and STD for savings and time deposits held by the private sector the currency ratios that appear in this table are defined as follows:

$$c_1 = \frac{C}{C + DD} \qquad c_2 = \frac{C}{C + DD + STD}$$

C. DD and STD are all data for the private

	1949	1950	1951	1952	1953	1954	1955	1956	1957	1958	1959	1960	1961	1962
AFRICA														
United Arab Republic c_1	48.95	46.69	51.29	51.91	49.37	50.06	48.23	52.19	51.35	52.89	48.33	51.96	57.94	60.97
CENTRAL AMERICA														
Costa Rica c_1	51.49	46.45	48.26	47.32	47.47	47.74	44.99	44.17	45.68	45.35	43.44	44.71	43.80	42.94
El Salvador c_1	64.05	58.97	57.89	57.23	55.28	54.51	49.62	48.87	47.71	46.85	46.40	48.30	51.95	50.05
El Salvador c_2	62.84	58.16	57.14	56.69	54.48	53.60	48.45	47.07	44.48	42.08	39.22	38.27	36.01	31.48
Guatemala c_1	68.90	66.04	66.89	71.43	70.26	69.97	60.32	56.98	56.63	59.14	58.70	60.43	60.52	58.77
Mexico c_1	53.16	47.18	49.98	50.68	48.44	51.83	47.55	48.15	47.98	48.50	45.96	45.65	44.88	44.00
SOUTH AMERICA														
Argentina c_1	51.59	54.01	57.44	60.03	58.48	60.94	61.66	60.00	61.87	60.99	59.38	58.98	59.23	61.63
Brazil c_1	33.16	32.06	31.35	30.23	30.54	32.34	32.10	31.06	27.95	28.24	25.37	24.48	24.55	23.72
Brazil c_2	25.46	25.77	25.61	25.16	25.89	27.79	28.28	27.82	25.38	25.81	23.52	22.60	23.08	22.69
Colombia c_1	53.02	47.89	46.05	46.21	44.06	41.45	41.03	39.65	43.68	42.17	41.37	40.72	37.63	35.61
Ecuador c_1	52.61	52.14	54.32	50.90	52.02	52.00	52.56	51.91	51.10	50.64	48.07	49.13	49.44	47.40
Ecuador c_2	46.11	45.46	47.13	44.51	44.67	44.25	43.88	43.20	41.90	41.83	39.60	40.64	40.40	38.88

a/ Using: C for currency in circulation outside the banks, DD for demand deposits held by the private sector, and STD for savings and time deposits held by the private sector the currency ratios that appear in this table are defined as follows:

$$c_1 = \frac{C}{C + DD} \qquad c_2 = \frac{C}{C + DD + STD}$$

C, DD, and STD are all data for the end of each year.

Table C-2. Efficiency Indices, $R_{4.}$ [a/] and $R_{5.}$ [b/c/], and Preliminary Statistics, $R_{1.}$ [d/], $R_{2.}$ [e/], and $R_{3.}$ [f/] used in the Derivation of the Indices, 1936-1962 [g/]

	$R_{1.1}$	$R_{1.2}$	$R_{2.1}$	$R_{2.2}$	$R_{3.1}$	$R_{3.2}$	$R_{4.1}$	$R_{4.2}$	$R_{5.1}$	$R_{5.2}$
AFRICA										
United Arab Republic	10.43	-	1.01	-	0.66	-	9.72	-	6.29	-
CENTRAL AMERICA										
Costa Rica	11.60	-	0.18	-	-0.09	-	1.59	-	-0.74	-
El Salvador	5.31	6.76	-1.18	-2.10	-1.32	-2.05	-22.30	-31.10	-24.83	-30.40
Guatemala	6.30	-	-1.07	-	-0.59	-	-16.93	-	-9.41	-
Mexico	6.98	-	-1.21	-	-1.40	-	-17.35	-	-19.99	-
SOUTH AMERICA										
Argentina	7.87	-	1.30	-	1.28	-	16.48	-	16.26	-
Brazil	13.22	12.86	-1.65	-1.13	-1.39	-0.96	-12.46	-8.75	-10.49	-7.44
Colombia	7.65	-	-1.58	-	-1.46	-	-20.67	-	-19.06	-
Ecuador	7.97	8.56	-0.11	-0.32	-0.31	-0.50	-1.40	-3.80	-3.90	-5.79

Arithmetic Mean	8.59	9.39	-0.48	-1.18	-0.51	-1.17	-7.04	-14.55	-7.32	-14.54
Geometric Mean	8.26	9.06	0.78	0.92	0.72	0.99	9.45	10.11	8.66	10.94
Variance	6.02	6.55	1.10	0.53	0.88	0.43	176.93	141.10	157.27	126.17
Standard Deviation	2.45	2.56	1.05	0.73	0.94	0.65	13.30	11.88	12.54	11.23
Third Moment	8.79	7.60	0.60	-0.05	0.52	-0.13	1,134.62	-1,032.46	765.48	-985.87
Fourth Moment	77.93	64.33	2.12	0.42	1.63	0.27	55,755.79	29,862.32	53,789.65	23,877.22
Relative Skewness	0.35	0.21	0.27	0.01	0.41	0.21	0.23	0.38	0.15	0.48
Relative Kurtosis	2.15	1.50	1.75	1.50	2.11	1.50	1.78	1.50	2.17	1.50

a/ $R_4 = \dfrac{R_2}{R_1} \times 100$

b/ $R_5 = \dfrac{R_3}{R_1} \times 100$

c/ The number following the dot indicates the currency ratio to which the statistic relates.

d/ R_1 represents in percentages the total length of the path travelled per year by the currency ratio from the beginning till the end of the period.

e/ R_2 represents the arithmetic average, expressed in percentage, of the annual rate of change when the currency ratio for the first and the last year of the period are compared.

f/ R_3 represents the arithmetic average, expressed in percentages, of the annual rate of change when the average currency ratio for the first three years is compared with the average currency ratio for the last three years.

g/ For some countries the period is shorter. For further information on the length of the period, see Table C-1.

Table C-3

Regression Coefficient of the Trend of the
Currency Ratio,[a] and the t Value[b] of the
Logarithms of the Regression Coefficients,[c]
1936-62[d]

	B.1	B.2	T.1	T.2
AFRICA				
United Arab Republic	1.00634	-	2.80955	-
CENTRAL AMERICA				
Costa Rica	.99796	-	1.08436	-
El Salvador	.98067	.97342	14.52828	11.93639
Guatemala	.99596	-	1.92197	-
Mexico	.98594	-	9.13634	-
SOUTH AMERICA				
Argentina	1.01923	-	7.15326	-
Brazil	.98566	.9444	7.21672	3.14893
Colombia	.98443	-	11.84595	-
Ecuador	.99888	.99698	.87067	2.16294
Arithmetic Mean	.99500780	.98828000	6.28523300	5.74942000
Geometric Mean	.99493960	.98822330	4.20813800	4.33205000
Variance	.00013631	.00011149	21.78937000	19.30133000
Standard Deviation	.01167532	.01055865	4.66790900	4.39332800
Third Moment	.00000112	-.00000080	36.91173000	57.70343000
Fourth Moment	.00000005	.00000002	859.99990000	558.81190000
Relative Skewness	.49310500	.45770210	.13170270	.46306470
Relative Kurtosis	2.57251100	1.49999700	1.81137800	1.50000000

a. The regression coefficient is the value of B derived from the trend equation $Y = AD^x$.

b. The t value is equal to the quotient of the log of D by the standard deviation of the log of B.

c. The index number following the dot in each statistic indicates the currency ratio from which the variable was computed.

d. For some countries the period is shorter. For further information on the length of the period, see Table C-1.

APPENDIX D

CURRENCY RATIO CHARTS FOR THE 1948-62 PERIOD

The charts displayed in this appendix are based
on data shown in Table 1, Appendix B.

CURRENCY RATIO CHARTS, 1948-1962

AFRICA $\underline{a}/$

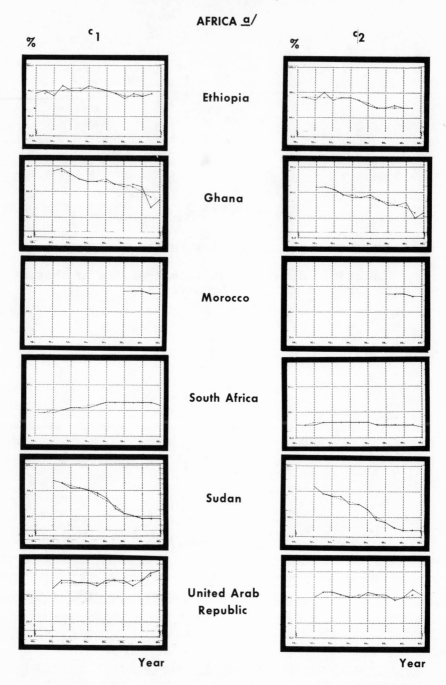

c_1 c_2

Ethiopia

Ghana

Morocco

South Africa

Sudan

United Arab Republic

Year   Year

$\underline{a}/$ The solid line represents the series of the currency ratio. The dotted line is a three-year moving average.

CARIBBEAN AND CENTRAL AMERICA $\underline{a}/$

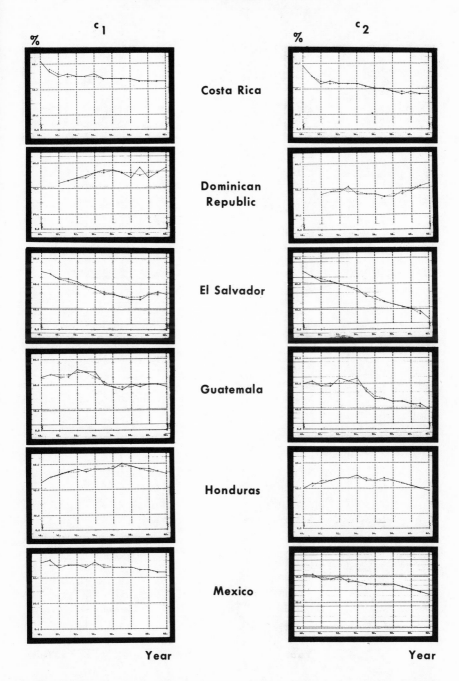

c_1

c_2

Costa Rica

Dominican Republic

El Salvador

Guatemala

Honduras

Mexico

Year

Year

$\underline{a}/$ The solid line represents the series of the currency ratio. The dotted line is a three-year moving average.

EUROPE $\underline{g}/$

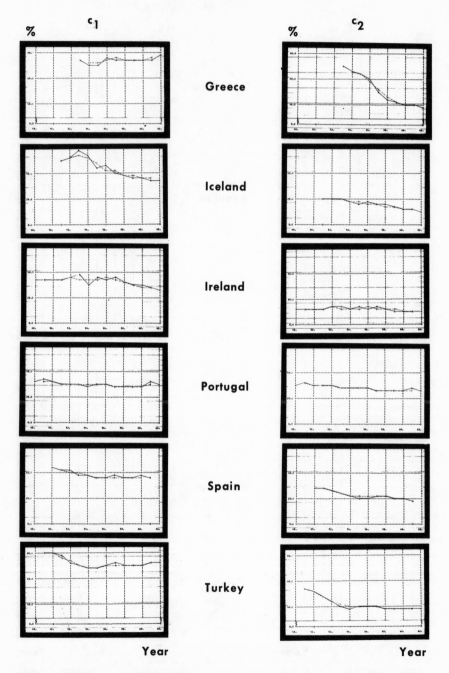

$\underline{g}/$ The solid line represents the series of the currency ratio. The dotted line is a three-year average.

MIDDLE EAST [a]/

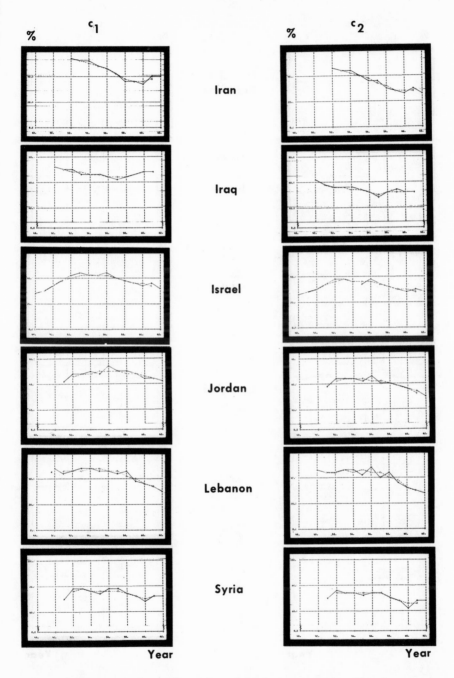

a/ The solid line represents the series of the currency ratio. The dotted line is a three-year moving average.

SOUTH AMERICA $\underline{a}/$

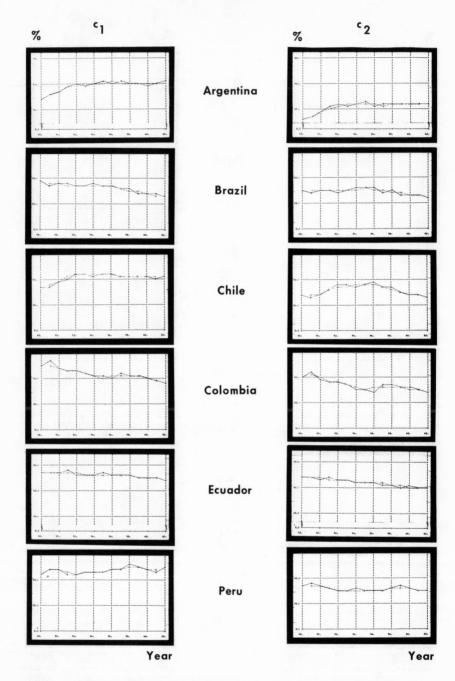

$\underline{a}/$ The solid line represents the series of the currency ratio. The dotted line is a three-year moving average.

SOUTHEAST ASIA $\underline{a}/$

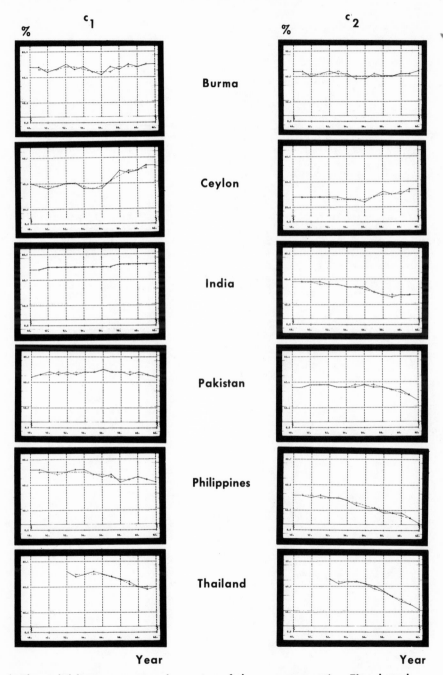

Year   Year

$\underline{a}/$ The solid line represents the series of the currency ratio. The dotted line is a three-year moving average.

APPENDIX E

CURRENCY RATIO CHARTS FOR THE 1936-62 PERIOD

The Charts displayed in this appendix are based
on data shown in Table 1, Appendix C.

APPENDIX E

Currency Ratio Charts, 1936 -1962

AFRICA

CENTRAL AMERICA

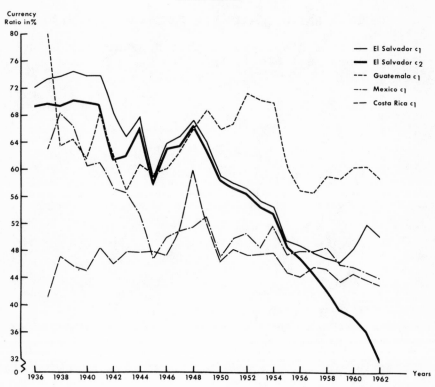

APPENDIX E continued

SOUTH AMERICA

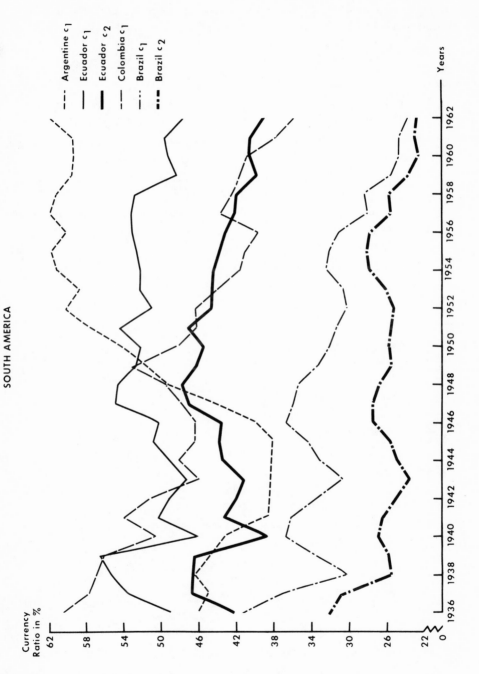

Currency
Ratio in %

Argentine c_1
Ecuador c_1
Ecuador c_2
Colombia c_1
Brazil c_1
Brazil c_2

Years

ABOUT THE AUTHOR

J. Daniel Khazzoom is Assistant Professor in
Economics at New York University, where he teaches
Quantitative Economics. He has also taught at
Cornell University and served as a staff member of
the International Monetary Fund.

Dr. Khazzoom received his Ph. D. degree from
Harvard University in 1962. Before coming to
Harvard, he was Economist for the Union of Co-
operative Consumers' Societies in Israel and led
its research on the introduction of the supermar-
ket in Israel. He has written extensively on a
variety of economic and social problems of the
Middle East.